T0066680

Geopolitics: A Very Short Introduction

VERY SHORT INTRODUCTIONS are for anyone wanting a stimulating and accessible way into a new subject. They are written by experts, and have been translated into more than 45 different languages.

The series began in 1995, and now covers a wide variety of topics in every discipline. The VSI library currently contains over 600 volumes—a Very Short Introduction to everything from Psychology and Philosophy of Science to American History and Relativity—and continues to grow in every subject area.

Very Short Introductions available now:

ABOLITIONISM Richard S. Newman
ACCOUNTING Christopher Nobes
ADAM SMITH Christopher J. Berry
ADOLESCENCE Peter K. Smith
ADVERTISING Winston Fletcher
AFRICAN AMERICAN RELIGION
    Eddie S. Glaude Jr
AFRICAN HISTORY John Parker
    and Richard Rathbone
AFRICAN POLITICS Ian Taylor
AFRICAN RELIGIONS
    Jacob K. Olupona
AGEING Nancy A. Pachana
AGNOSTICISM Robin Le Poidevin
AGRICULTURE Paul Brassley and
    Richard Soffe
ALEXANDER THE GREAT
    Hugh Bowden
ALGEBRA Peter M. Higgins
AMERICAN CULTURAL HISTORY
    Eric Avila
AMERICAN FOREIGN RELATIONS
    Andrew Preston
AMERICAN HISTORY Paul S. Boyer
AMERICAN IMMIGRATION
    David A. Gerber
AMERICAN LEGAL
    HISTORY G. Edward White
AMERICAN NAVAL HISTORY
    Craig L. Symonds
AMERICAN POLITICAL HISTORY
    Donald Critchlow
AMERICAN POLITICAL PARTIES
    AND ELECTIONS L. Sandy Maisel

AMERICAN POLITICS
    Richard M. Valelly
THE AMERICAN PRESIDENCY
    Charles O. Jones
THE AMERICAN REVOLUTION
    Robert J. Allison
AMERICAN SLAVERY
    Heather Andrea Williams
THE AMERICAN WEST Stephen Aron
AMERICAN WOMEN'S HISTORY
    Susan Ware
ANAESTHESIA Aidan O'Donnell
ANALYTIC PHILOSOPHY
    Michael Beaney
ANARCHISM Colin Ward
ANCIENT ASSYRIA Karen Radner
ANCIENT EGYPT Ian Shaw
ANCIENT EGYPTIAN ART AND
    ARCHITECTURE Christina Riggs
ANCIENT GREECE Paul Cartledge
THE ANCIENT NEAR EAST
    Amanda H. Podany
ANCIENT PHILOSOPHY Julia Annas
ANCIENT WARFARE Harry Sidebottom
ANGELS David Albert Jones
ANGLICANISM Mark Chapman
THE ANGLO-SAXON AGE John Blair
ANIMAL BEHAVIOUR
    Tristram D. Wyatt
THE ANIMAL KINGDOM
    Peter Holland
ANIMAL RIGHTS David DeGrazia
THE ANTARCTIC Klaus Dodds
ANTHROPOCENE Erle C. Ellis

Available soon:

For more information visit our website

www.oup.com/vsi/

Klaus Dodds

GEOPOLITICS

A Very Short Introduction

THIRD EDITION

OXFORD
UNIVERSITY PRESS

Great Clarendon Street, Oxford, OX2 6DP,
United Kingdom

Oxford University Press is a department of the University of Oxford.
It furthers the University's objective of excellence in research, scholarship,
and education by publishing worldwide. Oxford is a registered trade mark of
Oxford University Press in the UK and in certain other countries

© Klaus Dodds 2019

The moral rights of the author have been asserted

First edition published 2007
Second edition published 2014
Third edition publishes 2019

Impression: 4

All rights reserved. No part of this publication may be reproduced, stored in
a retrieval system, or transmitted, in any form or by any means, without the
prior permission in writing of Oxford University Press, or as expressly permitted
by law, by licence or under terms agreed with the appropriate reprographics
rights organization. Enquiries concerning reproduction outside the scope of the
above should be sent to the Rights Department, Oxford University Press, at the
address above

You must not circulate this work in any other form
and you must impose this same condition on any acquirer

Published in the United States of America by Oxford University Press
198 Madison Avenue, New York, NY 10016, United States of America

British Library Cataloguing in Publication Data
Data available

Library of Congress Control Number: 2019936257

ISBN 978-0-19-883076-4

Printed in Great Britain by
Ashford Colour Press Ltd, Gosport, Hampshire

Links to third party websites are provided by Oxford in good faith and
for information only. Oxford disclaims any responsibility for the materials
contained in any third party website referenced in this work.

For Theo
(24 February 2006–22 May 2007)

Contents

Acknowledgements

I owe a debt of gratitude to colleagues at Oxford University Press who graciously consented to a third edition. My sincere thanks to an amazing team of people including Andrea Keegan, Jenny Nugee, Rebecca Darley, Dan Harding, and Gillian Northcott Liles who support VSI authors throughout, and then arrange opportunities for them to speak at festivals and other public events. Appearing at the Oxford Literary Festival and the Cheltenham Literary Festival remains a great privilege, as does seeing your work being translated into multiple languages. Thank you.

As I wrote new material for the third edition, there was sadly no shortage of rebarbative and unexpected material to contemplate—including the election of President Donald Trump, Britain's decision to leave the European Union, migrant crises, indigenous struggles, climate change, trade and resources conflicts, resurgent nationalisms across the world, expressions of urban rage and ethnic hatred, identity politics, border skirmishes and illegal occupations, and social media manipulation. Even if readers disagree with my approach, I don't share the view that we are predetermined or even 'imprisoned' by geographical factors such as location, proximity, and physical geographies of the earth. Geopolitics is always contingent and dynamic.

I remain appreciative of my many colleagues (past and present) at Royal Holloway, University of London. Some twenty-five years later, it remains a wonderfully productive and rewarding place to research and teach. There is a wider community of geopolitical scholars, while too numerous to list, that act as a reservoir of immense goodwill and incisive thinking. But I am grateful to Associate Professor Chih Yuan Woon of the University of Singapore's willingness to review this third edition, and Dr Alex Jeffrey of the University of Cambridge for his editorial support. Finally, I also want to thank the Master and Fellows of St John's College, Oxford for facilitating a visiting fellowship for academic year 2017–18, where I was able to retreat and discuss geopolitical matters with my host, Associate Professor Ian Klinke.

Finally, without readers, there would be no third edition and no translations into languages other than English. Any author is always grateful for feedback—even when you know some readers fundamentally disagree with you. Thank you.

The third edition of this book remains dedicated to my late son Theo for bringing us so much joy in his brief life. Anyone who has lost a child knows how devastating and enduring that sense of loss remains, and having my wife Carolyn by my side has been indispensable to coming through the very darkest days.

Geopolitics

List of illustrations

The publisher and the author apologize for any errors or omissions in the above list. If contacted they will be pleased to rectify these at the earliest opportunity.

Chapter 1
What is geopolitics?

A shocking incident

Let me start with a shocking incident. In March 2018, in the English cathedral city of Salisbury, two people were discovered unconscious and unresponsive on a park bench. It was not immediately clear why this might be so. Within hours, the plot thickened, as they were named as Sergei Skripal and his daughter Yulia. The former was a Russian intelligence officer who had been granted indefinite leave to remain after he cooperated with the British intelligence agencies. They were brought to hospital in a critical state and subsequent investigation revealed they had been poisoned by a nerve agent called Novichok. Russia was immediately suspected to be the culprit. As one of the known producers of the nerve agent, it appeared that the former spy and his daughter had been targeted for assassination. Remarkably, after receiving specialist treatment for a month the pair survived. There was no murder near the cathedral, but elsewhere an accidental victim (Dawn Sturgess) of the poisoning died later.

The 2018 poisoning incident tells us something interesting about our subject matter—geopolitics. It occurred in a British city. If the Kremlin did sanction the attack, it was a flagrant violation of UK territorial sovereignty. It followed on from the blatant murder of former Russian KGB/FSB spy Alexander Litvinenko in London in

2006. UK–Russian relations suffered badly in its aftermath, and the Skripal affair merely reinforced that downward trend. Away from Salisbury, London is home to an ultra-rich Russian émigré community and its investment portfolios, some of which is considered by Russia to be 'stolen money'. Russia and the UK argue over what is truth and what is lie. They hurl accusations at one another. They accuse each other of meddling in one another's internal affairs.

It serves as a stark reminder to us that human lives, places, and objects such as poison and money are integral to how geopolitics can operate. Older readers might recall the poisoning of a Bulgarian dissident, Georgi Markov, in London by the Bulgarian Secret Service in 1978. Markov was killed by poison administered by a repurposed umbrella. The killing of Markov in central London was during the cold war. When it comes to the 2018 Salisbury poisoning some geographical questions remain opaque: how did the poison get transported to the city, who ordered it and where, and how did the assailants enter and leave the crime scene? Some of those questions were answered in the weeks and months that followed—two Russian military intelligence officers were held responsible.

So, we pose the question: why geopolitics now? We draw attention to a world that seems a far cry from the 1990s, when some were predicting the end of competitive/confrontational geopolitics. We never had it so good. The global spread of democracy, the triumph of market capitalism, and cultural globalization were going to make it obsolete. The Soviet Union and China, as the last bastions of communism, were scheduled for transition—and reassigned a capitalist and democratic identity. The 'end of history' was upon us. Welcome, we were told, to the brave new world of 'geo-economics' and the wealth creation opportunities of global neo-liberal capitalism. The transition was never quite as complete as was hoped, even if China and other countries have seen substantial improvements in wealth generation and distribution.

In Russia's case the shock of neo-liberalism led to rapid change with spectacular wealth gains for some industrialists and well-connected officials. Ordinary citizens fared unevenly.

More recently, the attack on the World Trade Center in 2001 (9/11) and the war on terror shook that prevailing Western confidence in the 'end of history' and 'end of geography'. Western states become involved in their own wars, mass surveillance programmes, and anti-terrorism operations. The economic crisis, from 2007–8 onwards, consolidated further a sense of discombobulation. In 2014, the American writer Walter Mead told his audience in *Foreign Affairs* that 'geopolitics was back'. Russia, China, Iran, and North Korea were all challenging the Western-led international order. But I think that what made this 'return' seem more dramatic was something that President Jimmy Carter warned about in July 1979. Carter spoke about a loss of confidence in the taken-for-granted qualities of the liberal democratic state. American voters did not want to hear his message but several decades later it seemed to capture the end of a post-cold war confidence dividend. The tenor of Western geopolitics is now markedly more pessimistic—barriers, fences, and walls are sprouting up all over the world (Figure 1).

What is geopolitics?

Geopolitics involves three qualities. First, it is concerned with questions of influence and power over space and territory. Second, it uses geographical frames to make sense of world affairs. Popular geographical templates include 'sphere of influence', 'bloc', 'backyard', 'neighbourhood', and 'near abroad'. Third, geopolitics is future-orientated. It offers insights into the likely behaviour of states because their interests are fundamentally unchanging. States need to secure resources, protect their territory including borderlands, and manage their populations. Presidents Putin and Trump would find geopolitics an attractive proposition. But they are not alone. Populists, ideologues, revolutionaries,

1. **The Israeli West Bank Barrier.**

and anti-democratic thinkers have been drawn to the straightforwardness of geopolitics.

Those three qualities are contestable. We might have competing ideas about what are the strategic interest of states, we might dispute geographical framings, and we can and do argue over geopolitical futures. The last of these can be backward looking and resolutely nostalgic—hankering for past glories and triumphs.

To help guide us through the geopolitical maze, I offer two fundamental ways of understanding the term geopolitics.

First, there is classical geopolitics. It focuses on the interrelationship between the territorial interests and power of the state and geographical environments. It is common for writers and statesmen to think of geography as fixed and deterministic, strongly shaping the political choices of leaders. The French president, Charles de Gaulle, even spoke of the 'controlling fate of geography'.

The second strand is critical geopolitics, which tends to focus more on the role of discourse and ideology. So rather than conceptualize geography as deterministic, the geographical is seen to be rather more fluid and subject to interpretation. If classical geopolitics focuses on territory, resources, and location, critical approaches focus on how the interactions between the human and physical produces 'geopolitics'.

Recent work in the critical vein has emphasized the more intimate qualities of geopolitics and made clear that geopolitics is not the sole preserve of states and governments. Where the critical and the classical converge is that both agree that the geographical matters; what separates them is how, where, and why the geographical matters.

If geopolitics does offer a seductive way of looking at the world it is often because it trades in simplification and objectification. Maps play their part. Popular framing devices such as heartland, pivot, arc, and borderlands do so as well. Before you know it, we are told that we only need a few maps or frames to make sense of the world. Geopolitics is sold as a reliable guide to the global landscape, and yet it uses evocative geographical descriptions, metaphors, and templates such as those listed above, and also many others over the decades such as 'iron curtain', 'Third World', and/or 'rogue state'.

Each of these terms is inherently geographical in the sense that places (rather than spaces) are identified and branded as such. It then helps to generate a simple model of the world, which can be used to advise and inform foreign and security policy making, and contribute to public debates about geopolitical matters. Geography gets imagined as a series of locations on which human events simply unfold. This becomes all the more notable at moments when change is coming thick and fast. But geography is not only three dimensional, height and depth matter as much as volume, but it also involves relationships and scales. Locations don't exist in splendid isolation.

Geography: more than 'earth writing'

Another term that can be a bit elusive is 'geography'. In his best-selling book, *Guns, Germs and Steel* (1997), Jared Diamond argued that European colonial supremacy, from the 15th century onwards, was grounded in weaponry, transmission of disease into communities which did not enjoy any immunity, and the replacement of wooden ships with steel-clad ships, planes, cars, and trains. Imperial domination is also enabled by advances in tropical medicine, infrastructure, and trading networks that facilitate long-term colonization. The work attracted a great deal of praise but also criticism for its sweeping generalizations and lack of agency accorded to those who were colonized. European colonialism, nonetheless, had a decisive impact on bringing forth global ecological and political-economic change. Simon Lewis and Mark Maslin credit this colonial contact as helping to usher in a distinctly 'human planet' and possibly the start of the Anthropocene itself—the moment the collective impact of human activity began to alter the earth's climate.

What geographers emphasize is a dynamic human–environmental relationship, so that the role of geography is not is reduced to simply weather and environment (such as the tropics and trade winds) which Europeans/Americans master as part of their imperial adventures. Nor is it simply taken for granted as a sort of unchanging backdrop to human affairs. The earth's climate has been remarkably stable for the last 10,000 years but not uniformly so. So, part of our challenge, when we think about the 'geo' in geopolitics, is to think about the varied ways that the geographical intervenes in human affairs, without simply concluding that things always happen somewhere.

Geography, as its etymology suggests, could be thought of as 'earth writing'. An activity that highlights the power of agents and organizations to describe space, to occupy space, to organize space, and to create places invested with particular visions and projects. Geography was and is integral to nation building and the creation of the modern territorial state. But the geographies of the earth, even in the modern era, have never been entirely stable and fixed. We had, after all, a 'Little Ice Age' between 1500 and 1850.

Geography is capable of change, as human–environment relations alter. Chinese investment in artificial islands in the South China Sea is a good example of how dredging and land reclamation are being undertaken for the expressed purpose of occupying and consolidating national presence while excluding others. Geography gets re-engineered. The Philippines, Malaysia, Brunei, and Vietnam are all adamant that China is behaving illegally and has no right to do so. Others such as the US have also raised concerns about freedom of navigation in this maritime region. But the end result is that China is remaking the physical and human geographies of the South China Sea.

When we speak of fluid rather than fixed geographies we could also point to the impact of climate change, which is ongoing. As the earth continues to warm so the physical and human geographies will alter, as sea level change makes some areas of the world uninhabitable and rising population numbers place further demands on the earth's resources. One fundamental challenge for geopolitics will be how to make sense of planetary change, and demands to exploit new and emerging frontiers in the oceans, polar regions, and even Mars and the Moon. Food, energy, and other resources such as water are likely to be under greater stress than ever before. The ability of the earth to support life let alone further iterations of geopolitics will be under ever more scrutiny. Welcome to Anthropocene geopolitics.

Geography is also networked and scaled, as bodies, places, objects, and processes are tied together across local, national, regional, and global dimensions. Susan Smith and Rachel Pain speak of this woven interconnectivity as like a double helix. Geography can act like an elastic band. It can be made to stretch and contract. Things and people can be brought closer together in forms of time-space compression but also be drawn apart.

Over the years, geographers have used shifts in communication and transport networks to make this fundamental point that there are dynamic relationships between flows and places. The geographer Doreen Massey spoke of power-geometry in order to make the point that places and people are made and remade in uneven and ongoing ways. When applied to globalization, Massey argued that places were negotiating global flows of money, people, and technology through a variety of digital and physical networks and relationships. Geography is not annihilated, rather places are shaped by uneven spatial relations and varying trajectories of activity. Internet technologies continue to link different spaces, places, and peoples together through an array of activities including cyberwarfare, citizen action groups, and internet trading.

Geopolitical and technological change is not always welcomed. One might wish to be resolutely rooted in past geographies and histories. Bureaucratic routine can play a part in reproducing geopolitical maps and visions. In South Korea, for the last seventy years, the government has maintained a series of appointments for officials who are governors of five provinces including North Hamgyong Province. The odd thing about these appointments is that the provinces are actually in North Korea and none of the governors has ever been to those areas concerned. And yet the five governors are all part of the Committee for the Five Northern Provinces. Unwilling to accept the legitimacy of the North Korean government, South Korea has maintained a bureaucratic architecture in the event that the armistice line from 1953 is altered in Seoul's favour. Amazingly, there are one hundred city mayors and nearly 1,000 civil servants attached to the committee. They are all salaried positions. It costs South Korean taxpayers around £5 million per year. The committee does do cultural and statistical work, but it is banned from making direct contact with the North.

Finally, geography is populated by human and non-human actors which play their part in shaping geopolitical encounters. Mobile resources such as fish stocks serve as a useful reminder of how a moving resource, which is not tied to any one fixed space, produces its own set of pressures for those seeking to manage it. For indigenous peoples in the Arctic, access to seals, polar bears, whales, and reindeer is integral to community well-being, and any interference by states and corporations is detrimental to the community. Sea ice and permafrost are critical infrastructure. Geopolitics can suddenly feel very personal when energy infrastructure projects or military investment programmes interfere with traditional subsistence harvesting. And when states and governments do engage in military and security projects, their impact is varied not only across space but also how it affects individuals. We don't feel and experience 'geopolitics' in similar ways—hence Massey's point about the power-geometries of place.

There are power-geometries to Anthropocene geopolitics, making themselves felt in the atmosphere, biosphere, lithosphere, and hydrosphere. As the world continues to warm and undergo further climatic and environmental change, it is not unreasonable to conclude that there will be ever more pressure to dwell in environments that are bearable for human life. Remaining cool and dry might become a major geopolitical driver in the future.

Advocating a critical geopolitics

This *Very Short Introduction* to geopolitics is one that is avowedly critical in nature and scope. It is not rooted in environmental determinism—we are not imprisoned by geography. Tim Marshall's *Prisoners of Geography* promises to explain 'everything' with ten maps. Classical geopolitics epitomizes that confidence that we can simplify global history and geography via a selection of two-dimensional maps.

Making critical sense of geopolitics means that we need something more. Ten maps is unlikely to be sufficient for one thing. Two-dimensional maps do a poor job at recognizing that we live in a spherical earth where depth, height, and volume make a difference to how we and others live and work. And there is a danger that if we restrict ourselves to only ten maps, we tend to privilege the rich, the powerful, and the largest actors in the world.

To take one example—what if we spoke of an 'indigenous geopolitics' rather than focus on great power geopolitics. Indigenous geopolitics refers to the manner in which indigenous groups imagine, mobilize, and interact with the wider world. The United Nations recognizes the rights of indigenous peoples (the United Nations Declaration on the Rights of Indigenous Peoples for example), and settler colonial states such as Australia and Canada have entered into land claim agreements and political settlements designed to recognized past injustices and future resource rights and cultural autonomy. While not straightforward, indigenous communities are in some cases substantial land and resource holders that are developing their political, economic, and cultural strategies, including working with international institutions.

Indigenous actors are not the only geopolitical actors. Geopolitics is situated within everyday contexts. We are all geopolitical producers and consumers. Geopolitics is embodied and experienced; sometimes dramatically and sometimes delicately. It is one in which objects (e.g. national flags) and non-human actors and forces (e.g. extreme weather such as the 'Beast from the East') give us clues as to how we make sense of our natural and human world. In Britain, extreme weather comes from the East and mild weather hails from the West. In my lexicography, I prefer to talk about imaginaries, sites, and spaces rather than 'geographical facts'. I would advocate an approach that does not fixate on territorially defined states, big powers, or particular agents like presidents and prime ministers.

If we do, we risk missing a great deal. We neglect the role of different human agents and non-human agents including animals, plants, weather, and ecologies. We might well underestimate the multiplicity of geopolitical sites that are available to investigate, including the home and the everyday. Finally, we need to ensure that a critical geopolitics does not merely speak, in the light of the above, to the interests of the powerful wherever they may be located. We need more than ten maps and we need different sorts of maps.

Linking geopolitics to popular culture

Geopolitics is multifaceted, multiscalar, and multimedia. It manifests itself on television chat shows, newspaper editorials, social media exchanges, and radio phone-ins. It is popular, moreover, in the sense that it is encountered and experienced in our everyday lives. Why, for example, has the adaptation of Margaret Atwood's dystopian *The Handmaid's Tale* proved so popular with television audiences? We might conclude that there are an array of sources and methods that speak to us about geopolitics. I mention Atwood because my favourite geopolitical sources are films, television series, and novels.

Another kind of popular geopolitics might be hidden and only comes to be commented upon when popular culture and media play their part in exposing it to further public scrutiny. While the film *Enemy of the State* (1998) imagined it years earlier, former National Security Agency (NSA) employee Edward Snowden dramatically exposed a world where some states such as the United States and United Kingdom spy, with the assistance and enrolment of internet service providers and communication corporations, on their own citizens and other people around the world. Snowden's departure from Hawaii, via Hong Kong and eventually Moscow, was headline news in 2013 and drew attention to a world where geopolitics and security were being shaped by the covert analysis of big data sources. Thanks to newspaper exposés, citizens discovered the existence of Microsoft PowerPoint slides explaining the scale and extent of something called PRISM. PRISM (created in 2007) is a massive data-mining programme operated by the NSA based in Fort Mead in the US state of Maryland. Snowden alleged that this activity was far more widespread than the US public might have even suspected and that communications companies were being ordered to turn over details of customer telephone and internet calls and search histories respectively.

A film directed by Olive Stone called *Snowden* was released in 2016 to mixed reviews, but it does confront the military-intelligence-surveillance complex established during the cold war and intensified post-9/11. The Snowden revelations suggest is that where categories such as the popular and the elite begin and end is complex. When the Snowden story broke, political commentators made reference to films such as *Enemy of the State* to try and convey to audiences what might be at stake in terms of surveillance and the sites and spaces of this military-industrial-communications complex. So, popular cultural artefacts helped constitute understandings of geopolitics and the leakage of PRISM created a series of diplomatic incidents as US allies such as Australia, Brazil, Israel, and the United Kingdom were forced to fight off accusations that they were complicit in spying on their own citizens in the name of the war on terror (see Box 1).

The third kind of popular geopolitics might be populist. It might be popular with some and unpopular with others. President Trump's mantra 'Make America great again' is a good example.

Box 1 A Chinese action hero: Leng Feng

In 2017, a Chinese action film was released called *Wolf Warrior II*. The film was a sequel to *Wolf Warrior*. Featuring the well-known Chinese movie star and director, Wu Jing, and a cast of Chinese and American actors, the film follows the fortunes of a Chinese special forces soldier (Leng Feng) operating around the world. Western viewers will see plenty of parallels with the movies made by 1980s action stars such as Arnold Schwarzenegger and Sylvester Stallone. The significance of the movie, *Wolf Warrior II*, lies in two directions. First, it was massively popular in China. It broke Chinese box office records and was the seventh highest grossing film around the world in 2017. Second, the plot is fundamentally about Chinese military power, as Chinese soldiers criss-cross Africa and the wider world hunting down arms dealers, pirates, and mercenaries. Chinese helicopters, ships, and advanced armoury feature prominently. With its special effects and skilful battlefield filming, it is every bit an action-thriller. In a movie promotional poster, Leng Feng accompanies a slogan 'Anyone who offends China, no matter how remote, must be exterminated'.

In order for America to reclaim its greatness, it needs to secure its borders, limit immigration, protect American jobs, and make sure the international security-trading order is not simply a burden for the United States to carry. For many Trump supporters, the vision of a 'secure America' was an attractive one—and one where presidential peccadilloes did not register. Trump is not alone (Figure 2). Other political parties and movements such as the Five Star Movement in Italy and Brexit supporters in the UK have also mobilized populist geopolitical visions and done so in an impassioned manner. Populist geopolitics pivots around how the state manages its financial affairs and immigration at the expense of 'the people'.

2. President Donald Trump.

The term *popular geopolitics* is used in this book to convey a sense of how geopolitical representations and practices connect to formal institutions and structures that make global politics—some of which might be popularized and some of which might be populist. In other words, Brexit slogans like 'take back control' which were so popularized during the 2016 EU referendum held in the UK underpinned a populist geopolitics. For Leave campaigners, departure from the EU would enable the UK to regain its sovereignty and regain sovereign control over its borders.

Chapter 2
Intellectual poison?

In 1954, the American geographer Richard Hartshorne lambasted geopolitics as an intellectual poison. During World War II, he had worked in the Office of Strategic Services (the forerunner of the Central Intelligence Agency) and helped to generate geographical intelligence for the US military. He, like other geographical scholars before him such as Isaiah Bowman, found geopolitics to be intellectually fraudulent, empirically distorted, ideologically suspect, and tainted by association with Nazism (and other variants of fascism including Italian and Japanese) and its associated policies of genocide, racism, spatial expansionism, and the domination of place.

Given this damning indictment, it is perhaps not altogether surprising to learn that many geographers in the United States and elsewhere, including the Soviet Union, were unwilling to enter this intellectual terrain. Within fifty years of its formal inception (and there is a prehistory to the coinage of 'geopolitics' including 19th-century writers such as Friedrich List), therefore, it stood condemned by a cabal of geographers, and more importantly by writers contributing to widely read American periodicals such as *Reader's Digest*, *Life*, and *Newsweek*. To claim, therefore, that geopolitics has had an eventful intellectual history would be something of an understatement.

How did geopolitics first attract such opprobrium? In November 1939, *Life* magazine published an article on the German geographer Karl Haushofer and described him as the German 'guru of geopolitics'. The article contended that geopolitics, as a scientific practice, not only gave Nazism a sense of strategic rationality but also invested National Socialism with a form of pseudo-spirituality. Both aspects were significant in shaping public and academic attitudes towards this subject matter. On the one hand, geopolitics was condemned as a fraudulent activity not worthy of serious scholarly attention but, on the other hand, the critics bestowed upon it extraordinary powers to strategize and visualize global territory and resources. The use of the term 'guru' was not, therefore, entirely innocent precisely because it conveyed a sense of Nazism being endowed with a supernatural spirit and wicked sense of purpose.

By the autumn of 1941, the *Reader's Digest* alerted readers to the fact that at least 1,000 more scientists were intellectually armed and ready to bolster the geopolitical imagination of Hitler and the German *Volk* (people). Frederick Sondern, writing for mass audiences in the *Reader's Digest* as well as in *Current History*, described a shadowy Munich-based organization called the Institute for Geopolitics that was intent on informing Hitler's plans for world domination. The author expressed alarm that so few Americans, even German citizens, were aware of these geopolitical geniuses and their cartographic and statistical scheming.

Such was the concern about this shadowy institute and the extraordinary powers attributed to German geopolitics that President Roosevelt commissioned a series of academic studies on the subject. While those experts were less convinced about the claim concerning 1,000 scientists and technicians in the service of Hitler, they concurred that geopolitics was providing intellectual muscle to German statecraft involving invasion, expulsion, and mass murder. What made the accusation of complicity even more damning was that some of the leading authors such as Haushofer were closely connected to the Nazi regime. This crossover between the academy and the world of government was crucial in adding further credibility to the charge that geopolitics was ideologically bankrupt and morally suspect.

By the time World War II was over, geopolitics stood widely condemned as being the handmaiden of Nazism and a whole post-war generation of scholars and their textbooks on political geography simply decided to omit geopolitics from their discussions. When one American-based geographer, Ladis Kristof (father of the *New York Times* columnist Nicholas Kristof), tried to resurrect the term in the United States in the early 1960s, he was castigated by his colleagues and damned for even mentioning the term geopolitics in print. Geopolitics, as a term and marker of intellectual terrain, carried plenty of baggage.

The origins of the 'science' of geopolitics

In order to understand the alarm and outrage felt by American critics during the 1940s and beyond, it is necessary to appreciate fully the genesis of geopolitics as an intellectual term. Coined in 1899 by a Swedish professor of political science, Rudolf Kjellén, it has often been taken to signify a hard-nosed or more realistic approach to international politics that lays particular emphasis on the role of territory and resources in shaping the condition of states. This 'science' of geopolitics posited 'laws' about international politics based on the 'facts' of global physical geography (the disposition of the continents and oceans, the division of states and empires into sea and land powers). Reacting against what he perceived to be an overly legalistic approach to states and their conflicts with one another, the introduction of scientific geopolitics in the academic and government-orientated worlds of the 1890s and 1900s was opportune.

As a portmanteau adjective, geopolitics attracted interest because it hinted at novelty—it was intended to investigate the often unremarked upon geographical dimensions of states and their position within world politics. Kjellén later became a Conservative member of the Swedish Parliament and was well known for his trenchant views on Swedish nationalism and foreign policy designs.

The claim to novelty is a little misleading and it helps only in part to explain why geopolitics became an attractive term and vibrant intellectual concern throughout continental Europe. Was geopolitics a 20th-century academic reformulation of more traditional forms of statecraft and state calculation, previously carried out in ministries of foreign affairs and ministries of war through the 18th and 19th centuries, rather than in university classrooms? But there were other intellectual contexts in which the significance of geography in shaping international political relations was discussed. The German writer, Friedrich Rich, is a good example of such an engagement. In his *The National System of Political Economy* (first published in 1841) he gave advice to German statesmen about the importance of geographical factors (e.g. the accessibility of a country to sea and land routes, the potential for territorial expansion, and resource wealth). Sarah O'Hara and Mike Heffernan have shown how many of the ideas associated with this nascent geopolitics were foreshadowed by government documents and press speculation. While geopolitics arose in response to specific late 19th-century concerns, it perhaps reflected more an act of academic colonization (in an era of major university expansion in Britain and continental Europe) of an activity previously conducted outside the academy.

Three factors contributed to the establishment of geopolitics as a distinct subject. First, economic nationalism and trade protectionism was on the rise as imperial European states such as Britain and France agonized over the shifting and increasingly interconnected nature of the global economy. The rise of the

United States as a trading power created further unease among these European powers. Second, imperial powers pursued an aggressive search for new territories in Africa and elsewhere in the mid to late 19th century. While imperial accumulation was on the rise, European powers confronted each other over ownership and access to those colonial territories. Britain and France were embroiled in tense encounters in North Africa, and Britain and Russia continued to jostle and parry in Central Asia under the sobriquet of the 'Great Game'. The famous British geopolitical writer Halford Mackinder described the new era as post-Columbian in the sense that the era of European exploration and colonization in the aftermath of Columbus's landing in the Americas in the 1490s was over. Ultimately, countries such as Britain and Germany engaged in rearmament, which provoked fears that conflict might materialize in Europe rather than simply erupt in faraway European-held colonies (see Box 2). Finally, the growth of universities and the establishment of geography as an academic discipline created new opportunities for scholars to teach and research the subject. The alleged scientific status of geopolitics was important in establishing claims to intellectual legitimacy and policy relevance.

The role of the United States in terms of economic and geopolitical influence further complicated these early geopolitical analyses of Europe and its imperial outposts. As contemporary observers such as Fredrick Jackson Turner opined, the American frontier was in the process of 'closing' as continental expansion came to its natural culmination. In the late 1890s, in the aftermath of the purchase of Alaska from Russia in the 1860s, the American Empire encapsulated the territories of Cuba, the Philippines, and Puerto Rico. Admiral Thomas Mahan, in his *The Influence of Sea Power upon History* 1660–1783, offered some sobering advice to the then Theodore Roosevelt administration. As a one-time president of the Naval War College, he was well placed to contribute to American strategic thinking. Looking back at Anglo-French naval rivalry in the 17th and 18th centuries, Mahan recommended

Box 2 Invasion novels and geopolitical anxieties

The invasion novel was a historical genre which gained considerable popularity between the 1870s and 1914. One of the most recognizable was George Chesney's *The Battle of Dorking*, a fictional account of an invasion of England by German armed forces. Others include Erskine Childers' *Riddle of the Sands*, which featured two British men on a sailing holiday who happen to prevent a planned German invasion when they chance upon a secret fleet of invasion barges. By 1914, over 400 books had been published about hypothetical invasions by overseas powers. Their popularity owes a great deal to the contemporary zeitgeist associated with Anglo-German rivalries, rearmament, and imperial competition in Africa and the Mediterranean. Public fears about 'foreigners' and German spy networks grew accordingly.

Invasion novels were also popular in Japan and emerged at a time when the Japanese confronted the Russians in 1904 for dominance of East Asia. In the United States, H. Irving Hancock wrote of an invasion by German forces and the occupation of the Northeastern Seaboard. American forces eventually repel the attackers.

that the acquisition of naval power was the single most important factor in determining a nation's geopolitical power. Sea power was the 'handmaiden of expansion' and an expansionist United States would need to be able not only to project its power across the vast Atlantic and Pacific Oceans but also to have the capacity to deter and/or defeat any rivals. The main threat, according to Mahan, lay with the German and Russian Empires and their maritime ambitions. His work was later to be translated and read with great enthusiasm in Germany and played a part in shaping German geopolitical thinking in the 1920s and 1930s, especially in the development of pan-regional theorizing.

The writings of Kjellén initially attracted swift attention from German scholars, who explored in detail the relationship between politics and geography on a variety of geographical scales. In part, this movement of ideas owes much to geographical proximity and the interchange between German and Scandinavian scholars. German writers were, like Kjellén, deeply interested in conceptualizing the state according to its territorial and resource needs. Informed by variants of social Darwinism, the struggle of states and their human creators was emphasized, as was the need to secure the 'fittest' states and peoples. According to Friedrich Ratzel, professor of geography at the University of Leipzig, the state should be conceptualized as a super-organism, which exists in a world characterized by struggle and uncertainty. Trained in the natural sciences and conversant with the intellectual legacy associated with Charles Darwin and Jean-Baptiste Lamarck, Ratzel believed that the state was a geopolitical force rooted in and shaped by the natural environment. In order to prosper, let alone survive, in these testing circumstances, states needed to acquire territory and resources.

In his book, *The Sea as a Source of the Greatness of a People*, Ratzel identified both the land and sea as providing opportunities and physical pathways for territorial expansion and eventual consolidation. A strong and successful state would never be satisfied by existing limits and would seek to expand territorially and secure 'living space'. Rival states would also seek such spaces so, according to Ratzel, any state seeking to expand would be engaged in a ceaseless cycle of growth and decline. The search for living space was in effect a fundamental and unchangeable geopolitical law—quite literally a fact of life on earth. He was, unsurprisingly, a passionate advocate of a German empire and for a strong navy capable of protecting its overseas interests.

For many other writers as well, Germany's geographical location and historical experience at the centre of Europe was both a blessing and a curse—it had the potential to dominate the European continent but was also a victim of territorial loss and misfortune. Germany was, as Michael Korinman noted in 1990, 'a land of geographers', with some of the first established university faculties dedicated to teaching geography. On the eve of World War I, German geographers such as Naumann and Partsch advocated a German alliance with the Austro-Hungarian Empire and a strong naval presence in order to expand its commercial objectives and territorial portfolio. With defeat in 1918 came the crushing realization that those ambitions were not likely to be achieved in the near future. The 1919 Peace Conference and the devastating financial and territorial settlement contained within the Treaty of Versailles sowed the seeds of resentment. When in the inter-war period the ideas of Ratzel were resurrected, geographers in France such as Paul Vidal de la Blache worried that these ideas concerning the state as a super-organism could be deployed to justify a resurgent Germany, determined to extract revenge for its earlier territorial and ethnic dismemberment.

Elsewhere in Europe, geographers and military officers were engaging with geopolitical ideas and relating them to a broader discussion on colonialism, national regeneration, and imperial mission. In Portugal, for instance, the emergence of Salazar's regime in the early 1930s precipitated public displays and engagements with Portugal's mission in regard to the wider Portuguese-speaking world. In Italy, the new journal *Geopolitica* was created in order to facilitate further discussion over Italian geopolitical ambitions in the Mediterranean and Africa. In both countries, new maps were circulated in school textbooks and public murals with the purpose of instructing citizens about the geographical aspirations of these countries. In Spain, geopolitical discussion concentrated on Spanish colonial ambitions in North Africa and the government was anxious to project military power accordingly. Unlike in Germany, Iberian geopolitical engagements were primarily preoccupied with colonial territories rather than reshaping the map of continental Europe.

When fears concerning a German military renaissance proved justifiable, the British geopolitical writer Mackinder advocated a Midland Ocean Alliance with the United States in order to counter any possible alliance between a resurgent Germany and the new Soviet Union. Suggested in 1924, it is often understood to be one of the earliest proposals for a strategic alliance, which was later to be initiated by the North Atlantic Treaty Organization (NATO) in April 1949. Although West Germany was an important cold war ally of the United States and Britain in the late 1940s, inter-war German geopolitical discourse was preoccupied with German territorial growth and restoration as well as cultural hegemony.

Geopolitics and Nazism

Geopolitics attracted and continues to attract the attention of ideologues and populists, and mass media allowed for the diffusion of messaging in the 1920s and 1930s. The most controversial element in the 20th-century history of geopolitics comes with its alleged association with Nazism and Hitler's plans for global domination. The idea of a state being considered as a super-organism, and moreover requiring 'living space' (*Lebensraum*), provided a dangerous if not wholly original backdrop to inter-war engagements with geopolitical ideas.

For one thing, the notion of the state as an organism encouraged a view of the world that focused on how to preserve national self-interest in an ultra-competitive environment comprising other rapacious states. Given the apparent stakes, the maintenance of the organism becomes critical and anything or anyone that threatens the healthy integrity of the state would need to be addressed with some vigour. Internally, therefore, those that control the state need to be vigilant. Externally, the health of the state is said to depend upon the relentless acquisition of territory and resources. Again, this kind of thinking tends to promote a view of the world which inevitably cherishes a well-equipped military force ready and willing to act when the need arises (an idea that was to be taken up with great enthusiasm in other parts of the world, particularly by post-1945 Latin American military regimes). It also promotes a moral detachment because these geopolitical writers are considered to be simply reporting back on certain geographical realities that are removed from social and political intervention.

Critics have contended that Nazis such as Rudolf Hess and even Adolf Hitler deployed geopolitical insights and perspectives in order to promote and legitimate German expansionism in the 1930s and 1940s at the murderous expense of ethnic communities within Germany (the Jewish community being the most obvious) and what the American historian, Timothy Snyder, describes as the 'bloodlands' of Central and Eastern Europe, especially Poland and Ukraine.

This association between geopolitics and Nazism remains much contested and relies in part on guilt by association. The notion of association is significant—it refers both to an intellectual connection, but more significantly to a personal bond between some leading German geographers and highly placed Nazis. Hitler and his associates, such as Himmler and Hess, used geopolitical framings to legitimate racism, territorial acquisition, and murderous anti-Semitism, as Germany was imagined to be under siege by hostile forces.

At the heart of this accusation concerning the intellectual and political connections between geopolitics and Nazism lie the writings and social networks of Professor Karl Haushofer. Born in 1869, he entered the German army and finally retired in 1919 with the rank of major general. During his period of military service, he was sent to Japan in order to study their armed forces. While on secondment (1908–10), Haushofer learnt Japanese and developed a keen interest in Japanese culture. His interactions with Japanese military officers and geographers were critical in facilitating the emergence of Japanese geopolitical institutes such as the Japan Association for Geopolitics and the Geopolitics School at the University of Kyoto in the 1920s and 1930s. He was and remains a towering intellectual influence in the development of geopolitics not just in Germany and Japan but also in South America, where his work was translated into Spanish and Portuguese and used extensively by the armed forces of countries such as Argentina, Brazil, and Chile.

After his retirement from the army, Haushofer became a professor of geography at the University of Munich and initiated the publication of the *Journal of Geopolitics* (*Zeitschrift für Geopolitik*) in the mid-1920s. As with his predecessor Ratzel, Haushofer (who met Ratzel as a child) believed that German survival would depend upon a clear-headed appreciation of the geographical realities of world politics. If the state was to prosper rather than just survive, the acquisition of 'living space', particularly in the East, was vital and moreover achievable with the help of potential allies such as Italy and Japan. An accommodation with the Soviet Union was also, in the short to medium term, wise because it would enable both countries to consolidate their respective positions on the Euro-Asian landmass. In order for Germany to prosper, its leadership would need, he believed, to consider carefully five essential elements, which lay at the heart of a state's design for world power: physical location, resources, territory, morphology, and population. If Germany were to be a 'space-hopping' state rather than 'space-bound', it would need to understand and act upon its territorial and resource potential.

Haushofer also promoted the idea of a theory of pan-regions, which posited that Germany and other powerful states such as Japan should develop their own economic and geographical hinterlands free from interference with one another. In order for Germany to dominate part of the Euro-Asian landmass, an accommodation with the Soviet Union was essential, as was a modus operandi with Britain, which was understood to be in control of Africa. Haushofer's prime geographical orientation was towards the East and he was an enthusiastic supporter of plans to develop a Berlin–Baghdad railway, which would enable Germany to project its influence in the Middle East and Central Asia. If developed, the railway would have facilitated access to oil supplies and (the British feared) a platform to disrupt trade to and from Asia. While the 1919 Peace Conference terminated German ambitions to pursue such a scheme, Haushofer's idea of pan-regions appealed to eastward-looking nationalists and industrialists eager to exploit the raw materials held in German colonies outside Europe.

While his ideas have been seen as intellectually underpinning Hitler's project of spatial expansionism and genocidal violence, Haushofer's friendship with Rudolf Hess and his high-level involvement in German–Japanese negotiations in the 1930s and 1940s was judged to be notable. Before his appointment as Hitler's private secretary and later deputy in the Nazi party, Hess was a student of Haushofer at the University of Munich. In his work *Mein Kampf*, Hitler evokes terms such as *Lebensraum* to expound upon his belief that Germany needed to reverse the 1919 Treaty of Versailles, and seek a new geographical destiny involving Central and Eastern Europe.

There is, however, a critical difference between the two men. Unlike Haushofer, who was largely preoccupied with spatial relationships and the organic state, Hitler placed a far greater emphasis on the role of people (in his case the Aryan race) in determining the course of history and geography. In other words, Hitler's obsession with race and his hatred of German and European Jewry did not find any intellectual inspiration from the writings of Haushofer. If the two agreed on anything, it was that the German state was a super-organism that needed 'living space' and associated territorial outlets. Despite his connections with Nazi officials, Haushofer's influence was on the wane by the late 1930s and early 1940s. He neither believed, as many Nazis did, that an international cabal of Jews and communists was plotting to take over the world nor endorsed Hitler's obsession with the undue influence of German Jewry on the national welfare of Germany itself. The failure to conquer the Soviet Union in 1941 led Hitler and his cabal to abandon the idea of mass deportation of German Jewry and instead turn to mass extermination in occupied Poland.

By 1941–2, German émigré intellectuals such as Hans Weigert, Andreas Dorpalen, Andrew Gyorgy, and Robert Strausz-Hupe had firmly implanted in the American imagination that German *Geopolitik* was Nazism's scientific partner in crime. Just as Haushofer was accused of being the evil genius behind the Nazi menace, his position and influence was actually in decline. Furthermore, he thought that the German invasion of the Soviet Union in 1941 was strategically misguided and his close relationship with Rudolf Hess became a liability when it was discovered that Hess had secretly flown to Scotland in the same year in an attempt to seek peace with Britain. While the origins of Hess's mission are still unclear, it marked a turning point in the alleged influence of German geopolitical thinking on Hitler and his associates.

Haushofer committed suicide in 1946 after learning that his son Albrecht had been executed in April 1945 for his part in the bomb plot to kill Hitler in July 1944. One person who discussed geopolitical ideas with Haushofer was the American colonel and Jesuit priest, Father Edmund Walsh. Interested in German and Soviet geopolitical writings, Walsh determined that Haushofer should not be indicted for war crimes even if he, like those aforementioned German émigré writers, was convinced that Haushofer was the 'brains-trust' of Hitler. Given Walsh's detailed interrogation of Haushofer in 1945, his academic judgement carried some considerable weight, but he stopped short of blaming Haushofer's intellectual corpus and personal relationships for Hitler's racist and expansionist spatial theories and policies.

Post-war decline in the United States

Having earned opprobrium from distinguished observers such as Edmund Walsh, who became the dean of the School of Foreign Service at Georgetown University, it is not surprising that the reputation of geopolitics was in tatters. A new generation of American political geographers spurned the term and instead concentrated on developing political geography, which was carefully distinguished as intellectually objective and less deterministic with regard to the influence of environmental factors on the behaviour of states. Geopolitics was not to be normalized.

In his important review of post-war Anglophone geopolitics, Leslie Hepple contends that the term 'geopolitics' dropped out of circulation of American political and popular life between 1945 and 1970. With very few exceptions, such as the Czech-born professor of sociology at the University of Bridgeport, Joseph Roucek, who published prolifically in academic and popular journals on topics such as the geopolitics of the United States or Antarctica, the term was studiously avoided. What is striking about all Roucek's articles containing the title 'geopolitics' is that he shows little to no interest in exploring the conceptual terrain occupied by the subject. For him, geopolitics is a useful shorthand term to highlight the significance of territory, location, and resources.

Despite Roucek's spirited adoption, very few employed the term geopolitics. The post-1945 period witnessed, if anything, the growing significance of the discipline of International Relations (IR) and realist theories, which addressed the role of the state in the post-war international system and rules-based international order. One notable moment in that disciplinary consolidation was in May 1954, when the Rockefeller Foundation convened a Conference on International Politics, designed to reconsider the 'state of theory in international politics'. This did not mean, however, that geographers and social scientists abandoned their interest in the geographies of the global political map. Geographers such as Nicholas Spykman (1893–1943) and later Saul Cohen (1925–present) recognized that the onset of the cold war meant it was more important than ever before to understand the territorial and ideological nature of the struggle between the Soviet Union and the United States. In his pioneering work first published in 1963, *Geography and Politics in a World Divided*, Cohen followed up an interest in Spykman's understanding of a patently fractured world.

If Spykman drew attention to what he called the 'rimlands' (defined as the maritime fringes of geostrategically important spaces) of Eastern Europe, the Middle East, and South and South-East Europe; Cohen's later work focused on so-called 'shatterbelts' (internally divided regions that attract great power competition) and attempted to explain where the superpowers were likely to be locked into conflicts over territory, resources, and access. The geographical regions closest to the Soviet Union and later China were seen as the main battlegrounds of the cold war. Conflict and tension in Berlin, South-East Europe, the Middle East, Korea, and Vietnam seemed to add credence to that geographical view even if the high-profile Cuban missile crisis of 1962 demonstrated that the United States was extremely sensitive about the geographically proximate Caribbean Basin.

Ironically, just as the term geopolitics was losing its credibility in the United States, Japan, Britain, and other parts of Europe, an argument emerged that American cold war strategy was implicitly inspired by geopolitical ideas. The National Security Council's NSC-68 document, delivered to President Truman in April 1950, warned of the Soviet Union's plans for world domination and possible geographical strategies for achieving that fundamental aim. Although dismissive of the Third World and its geographical diversity, NSC-68 was later to be supplemented by the so-called domino theory that warned that the Third World was vulnerable to Soviet-backed expansionism. Within a decade of the formation of NATO in 1949, the United States created security pacts in Australasia (1951) and Central Asia (1955), and entered into bilateral security arrangements with Japan and South Korea.

The few American political geographers such as Cohen who did comment explicitly on the cold war and US strategy were in agreement with general aims such as the containment of the Soviet Union, but anxious to highlight the tremendous diversity of the Third World. In the eagerness to understand the global ambitions of the Soviet Union, Cohen warned American readers that they should not underestimate the profound geographical, cultural, and political differences between the Middle East, on the one hand, and South Asia, on the other. American strategists, such as George Kennan who worked at the Department of State during the Truman administration, were, it was alleged, neglectful of those regional differences and NSC-68 was seen as geographically simplistic and overly concerned with representing the Soviet Union as a relentlessly expansionist threat from the East. So, the relationship between geography and politics was neither monolithic nor predetermined, and in a world divided you need in Cohen's estimation plenty of regional studies specialists.

Geopolitical revival in the United States

Former Secretary of State Henry Kissinger is often credited with the revival of American interest in geopolitics even if his usage was far more informal than that of the turn-of-the-century exponents. Kissinger, as a German émigré and intellectual whose doctoral thesis had analysed 19th-century European geopolitical history, was not typical of secretaries of states in the post-1945 period (Figure 3). He was an intellectual heavyweight in the Nixon administration and a keen observer of the changing geopolitical condition of the cold war. The context of the time was critical—the cold war was entering a new phase of relative

3. Former Secretary of State Henry Kissinger.

détente, even if the Soviet Union, the United States, and China
were still suspicious of one another's motives and geopolitical
ambitions. The United States was immersed in an increasingly
unpopular conflict in Vietnam, and Kissinger's use of the term
geopolitics was in part an attempt to get to grips with a new
strategic landscape. In the main, as Leslie Hepple noted, he uses
the term to highlight the importance of global equilibrium and
permanent national interests in a world characterized by a
balance of power. Eager to promote a new relationship with
China, he argued that Moscow's 'geopolitical ambitions' needed to
be contained and ideally neutralized.

While the United States strived to contain the Soviet Union,
Kissinger believed that existing American foreign policy had been
too eager to promote a military response to this dilemma. Instead
what was required was, in an era of relative American military
decline, an approach that was flexible and attentive to new
political possibilities such as developing mutually beneficial
relations with other great powers like China.

Although Kissinger's usage of the term geopolitics has been described as fuzzy and vague, it nonetheless according to some scholars repopularized the term within American political culture and led to renewed formal academic reflection on global strategy. In terms of popularity, geopolitics was reintroduced into discussions on cold war politics alongside a host of other subjects that sought to connect global and regional issues. While few authors possessed a detailed appreciation of the term's tortured intellectual history, it served as an apparently useful moniker to highlight the significance of geographical factors in shaping political and military developments.

Other leading political figures such as President Carter's Polish-born National Security Adviser, Zbigniew Brzezinski, were keen advocates of geopolitics and used the term to signal their interest in protecting America's strategic interests in an era of mounting global tension and, for those who were later to be called neo-conservative intellectuals, cited remorseless Soviet expansionism. The decision to fund and support resistance to the Soviet occupation of Afghanistan from 1979 onwards was informed by a geopolitical belief that further expansion had to be contained even if it meant that the United States and its regional allies such as Pakistan supported proxies in order to resist Soviet forces. Ideally, Afghanistan would become the Soviet Union's own 'Vietnam'. As many have noted, this decision had important ramifications in terms of inspiring the creation of the Al-Qaeda terror network and producing battle-hardened veterans such as Osama bin Laden in the 1980s.

One of the most significant offshoots of this revival of geopolitics was the creation of the Committee on the Present Danger, which used geopolitics and other academic pursuits such as Sovietology (the study of Soviet government and society, sometimes described as 'Kremlin watching') to contend that America had to be prepared to ditch policies of détente and balance of power in favour of a more aggressive approach which recognized that the Soviet

Union was determined to extend its domination over the entire Euro-Asian landmass. Disappointed with the more dovish Carter policies, the Reagan administration adopted a more explicit geopolitical vision of containment and dismantlement of the Soviet Union. American foreign policy arguably pursued Soviet-backed proxies in Central America and Africa and more forcefully supported anti-Soviet regimes throughout the Third World. If that meant, for instance, supporting Saddam Hussein's regime in Iraq and countless military regimes in Latin America then so be it. Short- to medium-range nuclear missiles were stationed in Britain and West Germany as part of NATO's attempt to dispel any Soviet attempts to expand their influence into Western and Central Europe.

By the mid-1980s, geopolitical discussions within the United States were primarily shaped by a group of scholars strongly influenced by political realism and a desire to maintain American power in the midst of the so-called second cold war (1979–85) following the collapse of détente. Geopolitics once more became a shorthand term for great power rivalries, and signalled the importance of the United States' pursuit of its own national interests in an anarchical world. United States foreign policy under Reagan was certainly more aggressive than under the Carter presidency and many intellectuals and policy makers associated with that administration were later to become members of the George H. W. Bush and George W. Bush administrations. Donald Rumsfeld infamously shook hands with Saddam Hussein in the early 1980s yet was later instrumental, as secretary of defense, in planning and executing the invasion of Iraq in 2003 and Hussein's overthrow and subsequent execution in December 2006.

Towards a critical geopolitics

About the same time that certain policy intellectuals were revisiting the term geopolitics in the context of the cold war, other writers were exploring a rather different conception of geopolitics. Later to be dubbed critical geopolitics, this approach was not realist in tone and outlook. As an approach to the study of international relations, realism has been highly significant, especially in the United States. It tends to assume that states inhabit a world which is anarchical because of an absence of a world government capable of restricting their actions. In the most basic forms of realism, self-interest and power projection are assumed as a consequence to be axiomatic. For many geopolitical writers, even if they do not refer to some of the high priests of realism such as E. H. Carr and Kenneth Waltz, they implicitly work with a model that is similar in outlook to many realists. For the Latin American generals preoccupied with their national security state in the 1960s and 1970s, the realist world view coincided well with a geopolitical imagination filled with dangers and threats from communist forces inside and outside the state.

For the critics of this kind of realist-inspired geopolitics, this jaundiced view of global politics tends to overemphasize conflict and competition at the expense of cooperation and détente. The inter-state system has demonstrated a capacity, perhaps surprising to some observers, to collaborate and develop joint institutions, international law, and intergovernmental bodies such as the European Union and the United Nations. Moreover, a new generation of writers, inspired by different philosophical traditions, is sceptical of the claims of realist-inspired writers to simply 'tell it as it is'. In other words, far from presenting a disinterested world view of global politics, it is profoundly shaped by particular representational schemas, which in turn reflect linguistic and cultural conventions. It is perhaps unsurprising that realist-inspired geopolitics has found a warm reception in the United States, where it is common for writers to present their grand designs for the world as if they were disinterested observers simply telling their audiences a series of 'home truths'.

First, we need to explore how geopolitics is made and represented to particular audiences. If we want to understand global politics, then we have to understand that it is imbued with social and cultural meaning. The current global political system is not natural and inevitable and the stories we tell about international politics are just that—stories. Some narratives are clearly more important than others and some individuals, such as the president of the United States and the president of Russia, are particularly vociferous and emphatic in determining how the world is felt and interpreted. Hence world interest in the State of the Union address is considerable, just as it would be for a comparable discourse produced by other powerful states such as China and Russia and their political leaderships. Would we be so interested in something similar produced by a political leader in West Africa or Central America? In polls undertaken in Europe and North America, we find that knowledge of the Global South and former communist countries of Europe and Asia is often patchy in the extreme.

Second, geography is either greatly underappreciated or perversely overexaggerated. The Andes, for example, is integral to determining the size and shape of Chile. Mountains, rivers, and rainforests have acted as natural barriers for neighbouring communities such as India and China. India and Pakistan continue to face off one another in the high-altitude environment of the Siachen Glacier. It is a punishing environment for human beings, and natural disasters such as avalanches have taken many lives. The two countries cannot agree on the ownership of this glaciated environment and remain at loggerheads over their shared international boundary (Figure 4).

Geographical obstacles rarely prove insurmountable. The American landscape was actively reimagined as a 'frontier', which underpinned colonial expansion and development by settler communities. The Rocky Mountains and deserts such as the Mojave were not barriers

4. Indian troops training at the Siachen Glacier, a region of dispute involving Pakistan in the Himalayas.

let alone imprisoning. The purchase of Alaska in 1867 from Russia proved extraordinarily important in the longer term but domestic political opinion was divided at the time. Having more territory and (potential) resources brought with it additional costs regarding infrastructure, security, and settlement. Expansion across the Pacific Ocean began in the 19th century and intensified as the United States confronted the Japanese Empire during World War II. Post-war US geopolitical and geo-economic expansionism reconfigured East Asian geopolitics and provided new opportunities for American companies to sell their products in new frontier spaces.

Third, geopolitics is entangled with ideas and experiences of gender, race, sexuality, and class. Geopolitics is fleshy and felt. It is intersectional. The everyday experiences of people and the strategies that they have to adopt in order to cope with geopolitical and geo-economic processes and structures need to be recognized as fundamentally varied. Concepts such as territory, borders, and scale take on a different meaning when considering war rape in the Democratic Republic of the Congo compared to the immigration of young men from North Africa to Southern Europe. If the global political boundaries are more porous to capital than to people, they are also more porous in general to men as opposed to women and children. As the feminist scholar Cynthia Enloe notes, global geopolitics needs to be linked to the everyday geographies of gender relations in order to better understand the differential impact of national boundaries, security, conflict, and migration. Feminist geopolitics is a thriving area of academic inquiry.

In order to understand better how geopolitics works, critical geopolitical writers have proposed a threefold division—formal, practical, and popular (Figure 5). The formal is concerned with the subject matter of this chapter. How do academics and commentators self-consciously invoke an intellectual tradition associated with geopolitics? Practical geopolitics refers to the policy-orientated geographical templates used by political leaders such as President Trump as they represent global politics. Political leaders use geographical templates to orientate their policies with audiences including voters. One notorious example was Trump's use of the term 'shithole countries' in January 2018 to refer to illegal migrants coming from Haiti and other poor regions of the world to the United States. While Trump denied using the term, the framing is revealing of a sort of world view that is indicative of how people and places are understood.

Finally, popular geopolitics includes the role of the media and other forms of popular culture, which citizens use to make sense of events in their own locale, country, region, and the wider world. All three forms are interconnected, as academic writers and journalists routinely share ideas and discourses with one another and both groups have regular contacts with government officials and organizations. They are also immersed in the media and popular culture. Geopolitical frameworks can help both individuals and groups make sense of the world for themselves and a wider public. Phrases such as 'axis of evil' and 'take back control' attract

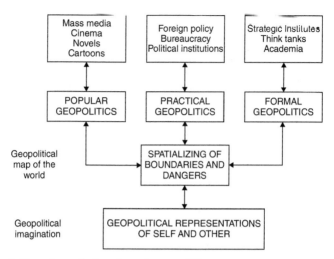

Mass media / Cinema / Novels / Cartoons → POPULAR GEOPOLITICS

Foreign policy / Bureaucracy / Political institutions → PRACTICAL GEOPOLITICS

Strategic Institutes / Think tanks / Academia → FORMAL GEOPOLITICS

POPULAR GEOPOLITICS, PRACTICAL GEOPOLITICS, FORMAL GEOPOLITICS → SPATIALIZING OF BOUNDARIES AND DANGERS

Geopolitical map of the world

SPATIALIZING OF BOUNDARIES AND DANGERS ↕ GEOPOLITICAL REPRESENTATIONS OF SELF AND OTHER

Geopolitical imagination

5. **Formal, practical, and popular geopolitics.**

attention precisely because they are designed to simplify world politics and locate friends and enemies. Presidents and prime ministers might use them initially (sometimes injudiciously), but these kinds of grand spatial abstractions provoke and promote discussions among journalists, pundits, and reading and listening public audiences (Figure 5).

The political geographer, Gearóid Ó Tuathail, has argued that this tripartite schema resides within geopolitical cultures, which shapes a state's encounter with the world. Britain's physical location on the edge of Europe, while it should not be seen as predetermining particular policy outcomes such as a commitment to the European integrative process, has clearly been significant in shaping cultural interpretations of geographical location. Also significant have been wartime experiences when Britain was forced to defend its national territories from German forces, including bombing raids and rocket attacks associated with the Blitz. In popular geopolitical terms, it remains striking how profoundly the legacy of World War II remains as books, films, television and radio programmes, and exhibitions continue to explore and review Britain's wartime efforts and the role of leaders such as Winston Churchill.

British prime ministers have for much of the post-1945 era placed their faith in maintaining a special relationship with the United States (American Britain), at the expense of a geopolitical tradition based on engagement with what might be termed a European Britain (see Box 3).

Likewise, if we wished to understand Russian geopolitical cultures better, we would need to appreciate, as the geographer Mark Bassin noted, how political leaders and journalists have invoked three separate geopolitical traditions. First, the notion that Russia is a part of Europe and that the country needs to embrace Western models of social and economic development. Second, Russia is a distinctive Euro-Asian territory, with its own particular form of state and society. Finally, Russia, like Britain, is a 'bridge', in this case between Europe and Asia. At certain times, a particular geopolitical tradition might be dominant over others. President Vladimir Putin is committed to restoring Russia as a great power, with control over its 'near abroad', a term used in Russian geopolitical lexicography to refer those neighbouring territories that were once part of the Soviet-era sphere of interest.

Throughout the intellectual history of geopolitics, there are examples of individuals and groups committed to different forms of cultural and historical analysis, such as those found in critical geopolitics today. The work of Yves Lacoste and his Parisian colleagues deserves some mention because Lacoste was one of the first to really consider how geopolitics was a form of political and strategic knowledge. He penned a book in 1976, with the arresting English-language title of *Geography is, Above All, Concerned with the Making of War*, which followed an earlier interest in the way

Box 3 Global Britain and Brexit

In June 2016 Britain voted via popular referendum to leave the European Union. In a bitterly fought contest, 52 per cent voted to leave compared with 48 per cent to remain. In 2017 the decision was taken to trigger Article 50 and begin the process of withdrawal. Opinion remains divided as to the long-term implications of Brexit. The Conservative government under Prime Minister Teresa May has posited 'Global Britain' to replace American Britain/European Britain. The Commonwealth and Anglosphere have been used to reimagine a UK operating in a new geopolitical and trading sphere—leveraging the advantages of English as a global language, the City of London, common law traditions, and cultural power. But did others invest in the UK because it was a gateway to other European economies?

There are challenges. After forty-five years of membership of the European Economic Community/European Union, UK infrastructure and trade patterns are strongly aligned with European neighbours—25 per cent of UK trade flows through the Channel Tunnel. The Republic of Ireland is strongly aligned to UK trading networks. European companies own British port and airport infrastructure, and are involved in UK energy and health markets. Global Britain will have to manage European supply chains and investment patterns while competing outside the European Union membership bloc with global powers such as China who are involved in ambitious 'One Belt and One Road' programmes designed to project Global China. President Xi of China rarely mentions the UK and Brexit in his speeches about China's plans for global trade and infrastructure.

American military planners used geographical knowledge of North Vietnam to target rivers and jungles in order to inflict ecocide (i.e. the deliberate destruction of local ecosystems in order to weaken adversaries) on the local population. He also examined the geopolitical theories of President Pinochet of Chile who was a former professor of geopolitics at the Chilean War College in the 1960s. The latter even wrote a tome on geopolitics in which he advocated the view of the state as a super-organism and arguably put theory into practice when he helped to remove the socialist government of Salvador Allende on 11 September 1973. American support was judged to be critical.

Lacoste argued that geopolitical writers needed to be more self-critical and play their part in unmasking how geopolitics was implicated with expressions of militarism and state power. His journal *Herodote* continues to be the highest-circulating geography journal in the French-speaking world and publishes critical analyses of contemporary events such as the global war on terror. Although Lacoste once observed that it was not good taste to make direct reference to geopolitics, he believed in a geopolitics underwritten by regional analysis (i.e. demonstrating an appreciation for local and regional differences) and understanding of the connections between geographical knowledge and political practice.

Any critical geopolitics worth its salt will be attentive to the fact that there are a wide variety of geopolitical cultures and traditions (see Box 4). New academic fields such as subaltern geopolitics highlight an area of ongoing interest, which takes seriously alternative geographical experiences, knowledges, and viewpoints. In so doing, critical geopolitical research is embracing an ever more diverse range of research methods and approaches, including ethnography, interviews, and immersion in communities and places that might appear far removed from traditional centres of power and dominance.

Multiple traditions

The final part of our brief overview of geopolitics as an intellectual term has turned again to the United States and the

Box 4 Chinese and Russian geopolitics

For those interested in Russian geopolitics, one of the most notable examples would be Alexander Dugin and his 1997 book, *The Foundations of Geopolitics: The Geopolitical Future of Russia*. Read again over twenty years later, it would appear to echo some of the tenets of contemporary Russian geopolitical practice, with an emphasis on the interests of Russian-speaking peoples and restoring the country's sphere of influence. It calls for Russia to annex Ukraine and spread disorder in the United States. Dugin has been described as a Kremlin-approved philosopher and strategist, although his popularity does wax and wane.

Chinese geopolitics, under the leadership of President Xi Jinping, might be described as more expansionist and committed to challenging the West's moral dominance. The One Belt, One Road initiative is predicated on China's infrastructural projects generating win–win outcomes for participating countries and regions and new geopolitical partnerships across Europe, Asia, and Africa. President Xi has spoken of 'renewing the Chinese nation', combining investment in military capabilities with multinational investment and cooperation based on 'sovereign equality'. Strikingly, for all the fears of China and great power rivalries with the US, the Chinese middle classes send their children to US and other Western universities, travel to North America and Europe, and work closely with US and European companies. President Xi's daughter studied at Harvard University.

English-speaking world. As I have indicated in earlier sections, this account needs to be complemented with a word of caution. The story presented here might be characterized as one of emergence, notoriety, decline, and revival. However, if this chapter had concentrated on the experiences of South America, a very different story would have emerged. For one thing, we would not have had to concern ourselves to the same degree with the alleged stigma of Nazism. In places such as the military academies of Argentina, Brazil, Chile, and Paraguay, which enjoyed a close relationship with the Italian and German militaries, officers continued to teach and publish in the field of geopolitics throughout the post-1945 period. German geopolitical writings were translated into Spanish and Portuguese at a time when American geographers were urging their peers to avoid the term and its abhorrent connotations. In a continent dominated by military regimes for much of the cold war period, geopolitics flourished without much formal concern about connections to Nazism and associated policies of spatial expansionism and the domination of place.

Scholars in the Soviet Union who still considered geopolitics to be ideologically tainted with Nazism did not welcome this revival of interest, especially in the 1980s. While there is far more formal engagement with the term in post-Soviet Russia, memories of World War II and associated heavy Soviet losses of life played a part in shaping academic reactions to this new engagement of interest in North America and Western Europe. Fifty years later, this stigma appears to have been lifted and a new generation of mainly right-wing Russian and Uzbek commentators have used earlier geopolitical writers such as Halford Mackinder in particular to consider their countries' geopolitical destinies. One area of mounting interest is the strategic significance of Central Asia and the emergence of a so-called 'Great Game' between the United States, China, and Russia. The United States and China seek, much to the alarm of Russia, to extend their military and resource investments in a region characterized by largely untapped oil and natural gas resources in the Caspian Sea.

The final point to reiterate, apart from geopolitics' varied intellectual history, is that the last section on critical geopolitics should not be misunderstood. Only a small group of scholars in the United States and elsewhere would describe themselves as critical geopolitical scholars. In most countries, including the

United States, most people using the term geopolitics have little interest in understanding that contorted intellectual history. Moreover, they use geopolitics as a shorthand term usually intended to invest their work with a kind of rugged (masculinized) respectability and willingness to ponder and report upon the grim geographical realities of world politics. US-based organizations and magazines such as *Stratfor*, *Bloomberg*, and *Forbes* often claim, in a manner reminiscent of earlier geopolitical writers, an ability to see the world and to make confident and concise predictions about its future composition, usually for the benefit of one particular country or corporate/business stakeholder as opposed to others. Social media encourages yet more short videos and podcasts promising to reduce complex geopolitical situations to thirty-second summaries.

Critical geopolitical writers aim to scrutinize those claims and, where appropriate, suggest other geographical ways of representing and understanding the world. This might include, for instance, laying emphasis on the human security and gendered nature of global geopolitics, which often means that women and children are more vulnerable and exposed to geopolitical violence and geo-economic inequalities. The gendered nature of global politics and geo-economic inequalities in the world trade system deserves further exposure. Finally, critical geopolitical scholars have a great deal more to do to think about alternative histories of geopolitics, including the role of indigenous and subaltern knowledges and perspectives. There are multiple geopolitical histories, cultures, and traditions.

Political geographers such as Jo Sharp and James Tyner argue that intellectual histories of geopolitics overemphasize Europe and the Americas at the expense of other engagements. In her research on East Africa, Sharp explores the writings of the former Tanzanian leader Julius Nyerere and his pan-African geopolitical imagination, which sought a 'middle way' between the binary geopolitics of the cold war. Moreover, these post-colonial interventions have been increasingly recognized as an explicit challenge to geopolitical theorizing, which privileges the understandings and experiences of European and North American states, cultures, and world systems.

In essence, subaltern geopolitics is not only predicated on exposing the Eurocentric nature of mainstream geopolitical theorizing but is also engaged in producing its own accounts of global politics, recognizing a shared vulnerability, collective interests, and past histories and geographies of inequality. Subaltern in this context never means marginal or small, rather it implies a critical stance towards those who would claim that their experiences and understandings should be considered universal.

Chapter 3
Architectures

The term *geopolitical architecture* is used to describe the ways in which states and non-state organizations access, manage, and regulate the intersection of territories and flows and in so doing establish borders between inside/outside, citizen/alien, and domestic/international. So when we speak of international order, we recognize that there are complex geographies underpinning claims to economic openness, international law, institutional development, democratic solidarity, and security cooperation.

Historically speaking, there have been a series of such geopolitical architectures which rejig the relationship between spaces and flows—sometimes literally through the control of river crossings, mountain passes, city walls, and other sorts of natural and human barriers. As we approach the contemporary era, investment in borders and border infrastructure expands. Modern governments, for instance, invest heavily in the regulation of their borders, as they provide the entry/exit point into a national territory. Such border controls also become a significant element in demonstrating de facto sovereignty.

In order to understand those shifts and the implications for geopolitical theorizing, we need to consider two fundamental subjects—first, the term sovereignty and how it informs the activities of the territorial state/border and, second, the geopolitical architecture of the 20th and 21st centuries, which highlights how states in particular attempt to control and regulate spaces judged to be disorderly and ungoverned. As the globalization of human and non-human affairs intensifies, so states in particular have invested more in regulating the relationship between flows and national territories and/or sought to strengthen their border security.

The underlying assumption of much of the post-cold war conversation in the West at least was that there would be a shared interest in managing the global system. Cold war geopolitics would be replaced by a new era of geo-economics (a term used to emphasize the intersection of international economics, strategy, and geopolitics). In this new world, trade policy, foreign direct investment, commodity trading, and foreign sanctions were more useful than military forces and nuclear deterrents.

But earlier expressions of optimism have changed. It is now more common to read about the return of raw geopolitics, informed by nationalisms and military power. American political scientist John Ikenberry argues that a two-centuries-long 'liberal ascendency', where political and economic self-interest forged a series of expectations and norms of behaviour, is coming to an end. In the era of Putin, Trump, and Brexit, it is no longer safe to assume that political actors are committed to an open and rules-based system of international order. In this pessimistic reading of world politics, geopolitical scheming is back because political actors are less committed to rules, liberal values, institutional support, and cooperation. Populist geopolitics has replaced geo-economics.

This chapter offers a more qualified reading around post-liberal international order because the underlying geopolitical architecture involving states and other non-state bodies is better thought of as being dynamic and highly uneven. In the post-cold war era, the way we organize our world and define the roles and responsibilities of organizations such as the United Nations and the conduct of states has been subjected to intense scrutiny. One danger we need to resist is thinking it is non-Western states such as China and Russia that are responsible for the crisis in globalization and the liberal international order. For critics of Anglo-American foreign policies, the controversial invasion of Iraq in 2003, regime change in Libya in 2011 (while claiming that military action was designed to protect civilians), and the war on terror are partially responsible for this erosion of a rules-based order. Rising inequality within European countries and the United States has placed further pressures on whether the 'system' can protect the interests of 'the people' rather than elites and/or immigrants. Wendy Brown reminds her readers that being sovereign may be on the wane as governments around the world struggle to secure popular legitimacy, and pursue 'national security'.

Is the resurgence of wall building and border wall projects indicative of an emergent post-liberal international order? One of the most powerful ways in which states register their determination to control or (attempt at least) to regulate mobility is by building walls and barriers. The wall may prevent the mobility of people and objects, but it also might help to regulate—to slow down, to monitor, and ultimately control. However, walls and barricades can be circumvented, torn down, and ignored. Walls can also generate a 'black market' economy involving smugglers, crime syndicates, corrupt border officials, and citizens from all over the world trying to pass through such barriers. Many will fail, some will be seriously hurt, and others will die horribly in and around such borderlands. Some of the most prominent walls and barricades include the US–Mexico border and the West Bank security wall, which has been declared illegal and is widely seen as an attempt by the Israeli government to either colonize more territory and/or make Palestinian communities less sustainable. These walls and barriers stand in marked contrast to the underlying ethos of the open system of liberal international order and globalization rather than iron curtains, protectionism, and security blocs.

National sovereignty and the international system

The ideas and practices associated with sovereignty and borders are critical in shaping the prevailing geopolitical architecture based on states, borders, sovereignty, and national territories. As Stephen Krasner has noted, national governments, while endorsing the importance of exclusive territorial sovereignty, have frequently violated those ideas and principles as incorporated into the founding charter of the United Nations. Apart from high-profile invasions of countries, state authorities frequently spy, survey, and carry out covert operations that violate the territorial sovereignty of other states. The United States has a worldwide spying and surveillance capacity thanks to specialist agencies such as the NSA and Central Intelligence Agency (CIA). But this does not make it unique. Other countries such as China, Russia, Iran, and Israel have all been accused by others of an array of activities including industrial espionage, territorial violation, and overseas surveillance.

Governments willingly allow their national sovereignty to be violated by encouraging certain flows of investment, skilled people, and ideas. Terms such as 'sovereignty pooling' remind us that states and governments might not always consider their territories to be entirely sovereign. With the enlargement of the European Union, the British government encouraged labour migration from countries such as Poland and Slovakia, and inadvertently might have actually provoked some British citizens to vote against continued membership of the EU in June 2016. The inherent tension in a world composed of nation states with distinct borders and national territories is how to administer and manage such entities when people, goods, ideas, technologies, and other things and objects such as disease are capable of crossing such borders and accompanying lines on the map.

In other cases, governments may appeal for humanitarian and/or military intervention when faced with overwhelming evidence of human rights violation and suffering. In the 1990s, there was support for the Responsibility to Protect (R2P) following the crises in the former Yugoslavia and Somalia and genocidal violence in Rwanda. Under R2P sovereignty can be violated if governments cannot or will not protect the lives of civilians. Sometimes governments might express outrage at sovereignty violations while secretly encouraging such an arrangement. US drone strikes in Pakistan during the war on terror might fall into such a category, and the 'outrage' being expressed as part of what we might think of sovereignty trading. In return, the US supplied Pakistani governments with intelligence and military support. In thinking about sovereignty, as a key if idealized building block of geopolitical architecture, it is helpful to distinguish four different types of interpretation.

First, commentators frequently refer to the international legal manifestations of sovereignty in the form of membership of the United Nations, the ability to negotiate and ratify treaties alongside the general business associated with diplomacy. At the heart of these activities is the notion that states recognize other states and therefore accept that they have an inherent capacity to conduct *international* relations. Even if other governments detest a state and its political leadership, that basic recognition is fundamental. In the weeks and months leading up to the 2003 invasion of Iraq, the United States and its allies had to negotiate and engage with Saddam Hussein's diplomatic representatives in the United Nations. In other cases, some states might not recognize the capacity of other states to conduct international relations precisely because they are considered to be unable to manage their national territories let alone engage with the wider world. Terms such as 'failing states' and 'quasi-states' have been used to imply that some countries in regions such as West and Central Africa can neither claim exclusive control over their territory nor secure internal order. In other words, Western governments frequently represent states such as Somalia and/or the Democratic Republic of the Congo as inadequate and, moreover, unable to regulate flows of drugs, money, and arms. It is important to recall, however, that some of the earliest geopolitical writers such as Kjellén objected to this excessively legalistic conception of sovereignty precisely because it neglected the fact that the geographies of global politics were extremely varied. So, terms such as 'failing state' acknowledge in part that the capacities of states vary even if they enjoy similar international recognition to others.

Second, we might consider sovereignty as conditioned by interdependence. In an era of intense globalization, it is unhelpful to presume that states enjoy exclusive control over their territories and accompanying flows with associated levels of mobility. Even the most powerful countries in the world such as the United States and China have had to recognize, in their different ways, that interdependence, while not eroding state sovereignty completely, has nonetheless modified politics and policy making. In some areas of social life, such as those encapsulated by national security, countries have attempted to respond to interdependence by enhancing governmental and, in the case of the twenty-eight European Union parties, regional control in the form of immigration control and surveillance while sharing or even conceding formal sovereignty in areas such as human rights protection and economic cooperation. This is sometimes referred to as 'pooling sovereignty'. It remained qualified as the open border region created by the Schengen Agreement never attracted full EU membership as countries such as the UK and Ireland never participated while non-EU members such as Vatican City are de facto participants.

Third, if we examine sovereignty in purely domestic terms, we can recognize some states are better able than others to exercise control over their national territories. Comparing the United States with the Democratic Republic of the Congo would be stark, as the latter has been consumed by a series of conflicts since the late 1990s, which have led to the death of millions, the mass rape of women and girls, and the destruction of villages. The national government based in Kinshasa does not exercise effective control over its large territory, and this has emboldened other countries to contribute to instability by funding rival militias. During the cold war, the country, previously named Zaire, was governed by the plutocratic regime headed by Mobutu (1965–97) and was tolerated by others such as the United States because it was regarded as a vital anti-communist ally in Central Africa. Mobutu was able to maintain some form of domestic sovereignty over the country because he used his well-funded armed forces (supported by exports in minerals and oil) to quell any form of resistance and unrest. This changed after his death in 1997 while in exile in Morocco.

However, even powerful countries such as the United States with well-established infrastructures and administrative structures struggle to exercise complete sovereign control. The control of immigration is one such issue, especially with regard to the US–Mexican border, which continues to pose problems for the federal authorities. The US Border Patrol, despite additional investment in personnel, vehicles, and sensory equipment, struggles on a daily basis to regulate the movement of people across the Rio Grande and desert regions of south-western America. In light of these difficulties, American citizens have created vigilante groups such as the Minuteman Project to patrol and pursue those who are intent on illegally entering the United States. This group, however, is not simply concerned with immigration but voices concerns over the status of Anglophone America and the growing challenge posed by Spanish-speaking communities in the south-west.

Fourth, other parties when respecting the principle of non-intervention explicitly recognize sovereignty. Developed by the Swiss jurist Emmerich de Vattel, the idea that states should be able to conduct their own affairs without intervention from outside powers is a vital ingredient of the current political architecture. For states emerging from the shadow of European colonialism, this was particularly significant in facilitating the creation of post-colonial governments. However, American and Soviet administrations frequently interfered in the affairs of other countries, especially those in the so-called Third World, whether in the form of military invasions, economic blockades, cultural penetration, political marginalization, and/or sanctions. For example, the United States invaded the Dominican Republic in 1965 and destabilized Chile in 1973 because it feared the emergence of further socialist governments in the Americas following the successful consolidation of the 1959 Cuban Revolution associated with the leadership of Fidel Castro. The Soviets sent tanks into Budapest in 1956 and again into Prague in 1968 in order to crush reformist governments. The underlying impulse of the cold war geopolitical architecture was one of spatial containment, seeking thus to restrict the mobility of people, ideas, and objects especially if originating (in the US case) from the Soviet Union and its allies.

In other areas of international life, many states have actively encouraged the qualification of the principle of non-intervention, as developments in human rights protection would seem to testify. The international community—as represented by the United Nations Security Council's permanent members—has not always responded so readily to evidence of massive human rights violations and genocide in places such as Darfur (Sudan) and Syria despite agitation from pressure groups, celebrities such as George Clooney, and other states outside of the region.

Some states are better able to exercise what they might consider effective sovereignty in the sense that they claim a capacity to control and administer their national territories and regulate flows of money, people, goods, ideas, and/or technology. Others possess greater extraterritorial capacities, such as the United States and China, and are thus able to conduct genuinely globalized relations. This capacity to interfere and engage with other states, other communities, and other regions was of course recognized by some of the earliest geopolitical thinkers. The post-Columbian era, as Halford Mackinder noted, was likely to be characterized by more intense relationships as states recognized that the world was being compressed by new technologies including transportation. Time-space compression has become even more intense and the term globalization has been widely used to encapsulate those shifts in the human experience notwithstanding the arguments over its geographical intensity and significance.

Geopolitical architecture in an age of intense globalization

Before we consider more contemporary configurations, what is globalization? The term refers to the movement of people, ideas, technology, and goods from place to place with corresponding implications for human relations. Since the 15th and 16th centuries, these flows have become progressively more intense, often with severe implications for native populations in what were later to be described as the First, Second, and Third Worlds. The Dutch, Portuguese, Spanish, British, and French were at the forefront of this global enterprise and the 'colonial encounter' initiated a global trade in commodities and people including slaves. Global entities such as the Dutch East India Company, assisted by their imperial sponsors, helped to construct and administer these trading networks.

By the 19th century, a new continental power, the United States, began to make its presence felt in terms of its flows of people, goods, and ideas alongside territorial acquisition in the Pacific Ocean and the Caribbean. As the global economy further materialized in the same period, the need for international coordination increased and the 1884 International Meridian Conference established Greenwich as the Prime Meridian and thus facilitated a new world map of agreed-upon time zones.

By the early 20th century, social, political, and cultural connectivity increased due to aviation, automobiles, and international trading. At the end of the last century, as the international system widened and deepened, geography in the sense of physical space no longer seemed to act as a barrier to human mobility.

For the journalist Thomas Friedman, the year 2000 was the high-water mark of globalization as software technology and the internet brought people and objects ever closer together alongside annual gatherings at high-profile events such as the World Economic Forum gathering at Davos. This bringing together was not necessarily a shared enterprise, and was one that certainly revealed enduring inequalities of access to technology, trade, and culture (Figure 6).

While the 'End of Geography', like the 'End of History', has been much proclaimed, the varied geographies of globalization have arguably highlighted the significance of borders, distance, interconnection, and responsibilities. Since the 17th century,

6. A placard advertising the 2018 World Economic Forum meeting in Davos, Switzerland.

European states, and later others such as the United States, have sought actively to manage the relationship between national territories and accompanying flows of people, goods, ideas, and money. The 19th century, as Gerrit Gong has noted, heralded the establishment of 'standards of civilization' that enabled European states to determine the current and future shape of the international system and the criteria by which new states achieved legal recognition via a form of 'earned sovereignty'. The latter in its many and varied guises is an essential element of globalization as it helps to provide 'rules' and 'expectations' for the global order.

The United States, as a so-called 'great power', has in the recent past been at the forefront of establishing a rules-based international liberal order. It was instrumental in creating post-1945 institutions such as the United Nations and the 1948 Universal Declaration of Human Rights. In the United Nations Charter, for instance, states accept that the Security Council has the right to determine what constitutes threats to international peace and security and that states must comply with particular resolutions relating to these. More generally, there has been a gulf between legal sovereignty and de facto sovereignty in the sense that 'sovereignty' has been abused, divided, and shared. States also attempt to protect and conserve their 'sovereignty' whether it involves building barriers, restricting mobility, or engaging in territorial aggression against others.

Citizens around the world have taken to the streets to protest about a particular geopolitical architecture, combining neo-liberal globalization and investment in security and mass surveillance. In late 2010, protestors in Tunisia precipitated a social movement, later dubbed the 'Arab Spring', which was credited with provoking regime change (or the threat of) across the Middle East. At the same time, social movements such as the 'Occupy Movement' were also increasingly active around the world highlighting what they called the '99%' of citizens who are being excluded from the associated benefits of globalization. Far from being a straightforward 'public good', contemporary forms of neo-liberal globalization were perceived to be beneficial to business and government elites, especially in highly stratified societies such as the United States and United Kingdom, but not exclusively so. At its height the Occupy Movement was credited with stimulating protests in over 80 countries and 900 cities and since then very few countries in Europe and North America have been spared expressions of economic and political nativism (a tendency to protect and defend the interests of native-born citizens), public disorder, and polarized political discussions around austerity, immigration, and wealth distribution (Figure 7). The onset of a severe financial crisis and recession (2007–8 onwards) added further resonance to these protests as governments began to promote the politics of austerity and retrenchment. Over a decade later, it is perhaps not coincidental that discussions of a post-liberal international order coincided with a structural crisis among liberal democracies in the West. Plenty of political leaders, across the political spectrum, have emerged to capitalize on this sense of dissatisfaction and anger.

7. An anti-austerity march in central London in February 2018.

If we want to understand more fully how global geopolitics has changed, then we need to examine how states, among others, have responded, resisted, and regulated processes associated with globalization. John Agnew speaks of sovereignty regimes and distinguishes between different types of spatial configurations and relationships between state control and authority that criss-cross national and regional borders. So rather than being a case of state sovereignty and forms of globalization being in competition with one another, Agnew identifies various forms of 'globalist states'. If traditional geopolitical thinking was preoccupied with states and the changing fortunes of European empires, then more recent writings have explored the role of non-state actors, networks, regional organizations, transnational corporations, and international governmental organizations. While states and concepts such as sovereignty remain highly significant, a web of interdependence and coexistence is changing international relations and the accompanying global geographies. It is now common to read that states possess multiple borders and that governance is expressed in a more global and polycentric manner, as institutions such as the World Bank, the United Nations, global media corporations, and the World Trade Organization (WTO) play their parts in shaping global behaviour.

The notion of intensity is important here because of mounting evidence that states have had to adapt to ever more issues and flows that possess an ability to transcend international boundaries and exclusive sovereignties. The list would undoubtedly include global climate change, human rights, drug trafficking, and the spectre of nuclear annihilation. Over the last sixty years, a particular form of global order was said to have prevailed following the defeat of Japan and Germany in 1945. Sponsored by the victorious United States and its allies including Britain, it has been characterized by three key features—the development of a global capitalist economy, the creation of the United Nations, and the promotion of liberal democracy. The United States was instrumental in creating a new economic order based on the creation of two institutions: the International Monetary Fund (IMF) and the World Bank. These bodies, first considered at Bretton Woods, New Hampshire, in 1944, would aim to establish international economic stability and provide funds for post-war reconstruction.

What emerged was something called the Bretton Woods system. It was intended to establish the institutional bodies and rules governing post-war commercial and financial relations. The spectre of aggressive forms of economic nationalism was to be banished in the process. At the heart of this system were forty-four nations who attended the United Nations Monetary and Financial Conference in July 1944. Once it had been ratified in 1946, each country had to accept that the exchange rate of its currency would remain within a fixed value banding so that the IMF could help promote and manage global financial stability. In 1971, the system of fixed currencies collapsed and the United States suspended the conversion from dollars to gold.

After 1971, international currencies were no longer tied to particular exchange rates and international financial flows increased. A number of world cities, such as New York, Paris, and London, emerged as major hubs of the post-Bretton Woods era. As global financial centres became more integrated and networked with one another, concern has been expressed that these 'global cities' have more in common with one another than their domestic hinterlands. In London, the internationalization of the Stock Exchange in the 1980s provoked an influx of wealth and speculation leading to inflationary pressures on property markets.

Bretton Woods was only one element in this reconstructive investment. The creation of the United Nations in 1945 was integral to the management and regulation of state behaviour in the post-war world. The United Nations Charter played a key role in establishing sovereignty and other norms such as non-interference in the affairs of other UN members. International legal agreements including the General Agreement of Tariffs and Trade played their part in sustaining a global 'rule book'. In addition, the promotion of liberal democracy by the United States as the preferred system of political expression was critical in legitimating their role in the ensuing cold war struggle involving the Soviet Union and China who publicly promoted socialist revolutions. As a consequence of the collapse of the Soviet Union in 1991 and the decline of socialist regimes in Eastern Europe and elsewhere, institutions associated with the economic and political imprint of the United States have effectively prefigured and advocated the prioritization of global capitalist development based on free trade, open markets, and foreign direct investment. Transnational corporations facilitated the consolidation of such a global economic landscape through their investment and production activities, supported and sustained by states and governments around the world.

All of this was occurring in a world where the legacies of World War II continued to make themselves felt. In February 1945, the Soviet Union, the United States, and Britain participated in a meeting in the Crimean resort of Yalta. This conference, involving Stalin, Roosevelt, and Churchill, effectively determined the fate of post-1945 Europe. The main outcomes were: the Soviet Union would join the United Nations in return for a buffer zone in Eastern and Central Europe; the Soviets would declare war on Japan; Germany and Austria would be occupied and divided into four sectors and managed by the three conference participants plus France; Germany would have to pay reparations; and countries such as Estonia and Latvia were allowed to remain under Soviet occupation. So all of this needs to be remembered when we speak of the norms and principles underwriting the United Nations Charter.

It would take another forty-four years before the geopolitics of Europe was to be fundamentally altered by the collapse of the East German regime and other communist governments in

Eastern and Central Europe. The break-up of the Berlin Wall (built in 1961) was one of the most memorable moments of that transformation. By the early 2000s, the Soviet Union had disintegrated, former Eastern European communist governments had joined the European Union and NATO, and Russia had formed new partnerships with both the EU and NATO. In the last ten years, EU–Russian cooperation has become more tense as issues such as gas pricing, electoral interference and 'fake news', the annexation of Crimea and instability of eastern Ukraine, immigration control, border security, and military exercises have become areas of tension.

The link between geopolitical competition and economic globalization have been much debated. For some, the state has been eclipsed by these intense demands of the global economic and political order. Economic institutions such as the World Bank and IMF are able, especially in sub-Saharan Africa and Asia, to exercise considerable control over government expenditure and macro-economic policy where and when states have requested financial assistance. So-called structural adjustment programmes have imposed accompanying conditions, which might include demands that governments cut public expenditure or ease restrictions on foreign investment. During the cold war, such international economic arrangements had geopolitical implications as US-dominated international organizations such as the IMF rendered greater control and influence over regions such as West Africa, considered to be strategically significant because of their oil and natural gas resources. Marxist geographer David Harvey has referred to 'accumulation by dispossession' to highlight the manner in which international institutions have facilitated access to Third World markets and resources. In other regions of the world such as South East Asia, international loans were directed towards states considered to be allies in the struggle against Soviet and/or Chinese-backed socialist ambitions. Countries such as South Korea and Malaysia were the beneficiaries in this regard, especially during the Vietnam conflict.

American administrators in particular feared that if Vietnam fell to communist forces then neighbouring countries would also be vulnerable to socialist interference.

Other commentators contend that international economic organizations such as the IMF or transnational corporations depend on their relationship with states, albeit one that has been transformed by global flows and networks. States ultimately created the post-war economic and political order and the United States was the most significant in this regard. Moreover, property, taxation, and investment laws both regulate and protect the activities of transnational corporations. The notion of a 'transformed state' is more helpful in the sense that it can be used to highlight the ways in which globalization has altered the 'state of affairs', including global political order. As the economic geographer Peter Dicken has opined, states continue to shape specific business and economic activities and regulate within and across their national jurisdictions. Ironically, there are now more states than ever, at a time when some observers have predicted the demise of the state as a direct consequence of intense globalization.

The implications for geopolitics are profound. On the one hand, the ending of the cold war witnessed the emergence of new states and regional organizations such as Slovenia and the Commonwealth of Independent States respectively. The collapse of the Soviet Union and the gradual incorporation of Russia and China into international economic bodies such as the WTO have highlighted how former communist/socialist countries are embedded, some more so than others, within the networks and structures associated with global capitalist development. The term 'Washington Consensus' was used to describe how the rest of the world appeared to be following the rules, norms, and values associated with a US-led international order. Ideas and policies associated with neo-liberalism, such as open markets and foreign direct investment, appeared hegemonic.

A deregulated vision of world geography would prevail—the globe as a border-free zone with unfettered flows of investment and goods. The state was intended to be a facilitator of business and some large US-based companies such as Enron were, at one point, well able to take full advantage of the relative lack of judicial and fiscal structures. During the 1990s, commentators such as Francis Fukuyama lauded the triumph of these ideas and practices associated with US-sponsored neo-liberalism and democracy. In other words, it appeared that the 'West' had won the battle of ideas and practices.

On the other hand, this story of triumph and assimilation was never quite as obvious. The democratic turn is not the norm in all parts of the world including China, sub-Saharan Africa, and parts of the Islamic world. Even when democracy has appeared in places such as Egypt and Algeria, for instance, it has not been embraced by authoritarian governments and the militaries of those countries. As the political theorist David Runciman notes, the fusion between liberalism and democracy is not axiomatic and illiberal democratic thought and practice also has a European provenance. The adoption of economic neo-liberalism has attracted a great deal of opposition in many countries in the Global South as well as Western Europe and the United States. Others now speak of a post-Washington Consensus or even a New Washington Consensus, whereby neo-liberalism attempts to resuscitate itself and promote changes at the micro level in areas such as health and community building, all the while avoiding questions as to why governments, markets, and corporations may be failing those very communities in the first place.

The emergence of anti-globalization and then anti-austerity movements are the most obvious manifestations of that resistance to the continued presence of economic and political neo-liberalism. In many countries, there is a palpable sense of rage against elites that failed to anticipate and manage the 2008 financial crash. The rise of populism serves as a reminder that austerity (a concern for the political left) and immigration (a concern of the political right) have contributed to expressions of anger about how the movement of people and capital are managed. While some wanted to travel in search of better lives, others feared that their jobs and well-being were being imperilled by new arrivals. The control of borders becomes axiomatic to populist forms of geopolitics. Civil wars and international conflicts place further pressures on states and communities to accommodate refugees, asylum seekers, and migrants.

The first signs of resistance and resentment against 'elites' emerged in cities such as Cologne, Genoa, London, and Seattle in the 1990s. Frequently coinciding with meetings of the WTO or G8 (the grouping of the eight largest economies in the world), anti-globalization critics are censorious of the way neo-liberalism has eroded national boundaries and thus exposed communities to unwanted interference from global corporations, international institutions, and/or hegemonic powers. At its heart lies concerns that certain kinds of flows are overwhelming local places and communities and that national governments are not able or willing to mitigate those flows as they intersect with territories.

The anti-globalization movement remains diverse and attracts political parties and organizations across international borders. Such initiatives were bolstered further by the initiation of the Occupy Movement, which was launched in October 2011 as an international protest movement against socio-economic inequality (Box 5). Inspired by the 'Arab Spring' movement and the Indignados movement in Spain and Portugal, there was growing interest in registering widespread protest against the concentration of global wealth and the corporatization of global geopolitics. The word 'Occupy' was important because this was a highly geographical protest movement. While its aim was to call for a recalibration of neo-liberal globalization and the interaction of the international financial system, it was also a spatial challenge. In the same month, protestors established a protest

Box 5 Placing protest: Zuccotti Park, New York City

Zuccotti Park, or Liberty Plaza Park, would have been unknown to most citizens except New Yorkers and visitors. Located in Lower Manhattan, it was damaged in the midst of the 9/11 attack on the Twin Towers. Renamed after the park was bought by a corporation in 2006, it had hosted a series of commemorative events in the months and years after 9/11. A decade later, Zuccotti Park was the site of an altogether different kind of geopolitical performance, one in which the city of New York (and the United States) was not being remembered as a victim of violence but as a producer of inequality around the world. On 17 September 2011, protestors gathered at Zuccotti Park to launch 'Occupy Wall Street'. The choice of the location was not only close to New York's financial centre but also a privately owned park that could not be shut down by the city authorities. The park's owners, Brookfield Properties, the city of New York government, and the New York Police Department then found themselves locked in a series of legal and physical battles to restrict access to the park and prevent the erection of tents and installations in the park itself. Such restrictions remain in place to this day but the protests provoked national and international debate, and high-profile individuals such as Naomi Wolf were arrested while expressing support for the protestors.

camp outside St Paul's Cathedral in the City of London. The choice was a deliberate one. The proximity to the financial centre of London was intended to highlight the close relationship between the UK government and the international banking sector, but also to ask questions about what role civil society and the third sector (including religious organizations) should play in the midst of ongoing financial crisis and austerity.

Britain's decision to leave the EU in June 2016 brought into focus debates about immigration, open borders, and control of governance. Across the political spectrum, British citizens and political parties appeared deeply divided over how Britain did or did not adjust to regional and global governance structures. But rather than being a struggle against globalization, it is better thought of as an expression of economic nationalism and anti-immigration. For the British government, Global Britain was a widely adopted slogan indicating not a rejection of the global but a determination that Britain not the EU would shape that relationship.

Neo-liberal globalization and the future of the liberal international order

How might neo-liberal globalization be connected to the future of the liberal international order? While neo-liberal globalization intensifies, with governments such as the US and UK giving ever greater emphasis to market accessibility and tax-friendly policies for business coupled with reduced state involvement in the public sector, the war on terror (2001 onwards) also precipitated increased expenditure in military/security sectors. As a result, concern has been expressed that the distinction between the domestic and the international is increasingly being blurred by transnational security practices, which aim to secure economic and political spaces in European and North American cities while containing the violence and disorder elsewhere in the world such as Syria, Iraq, and Afghanistan. In other words, there is a growing interest in how people, regardless of location per se, are policed and securitized. Of course, places still matter in the sense that the nature and extent of that policing and security work does vary and some bodies will be made more precarious than others, but in general is globalization becoming more akin to a global security project (Box 6)?

Social scientists, in political geography and allied fields such as IR and Security Studies, argue that the current geopolitical architecture is predicated on spatial administration rather than

Box 6 Urban rage

In his book, *Urban Rage*, the urban geographer Mustafa Dikeç makes a compelling case for considering how cities in Europe and North America have been engulfed by protest and disorder. Ranging from Ferguson in Missouri to London, Paris, Stockholm, and Istanbul in Europe, he identifies exclusion and grievance as pivotal. Expensive housing, racist policing, social deprivation, economic dislocation, aggressive nationalisms, and anti-immigrant politics are all considered to be toxic in their effects. Worse still, it is contended that local and national democratic systems are slow to react and at times indifferent to those exclusions and inequality. In some cases, such as the town of Ferguson, the local police force can and does appear to local African American residents as an occupying paramilitary force, and legal authorities appear intent on penalizing residents for infringements such as loitering and jaywalking. Such perceptions fuel 'urban rage' among the poor and vulnerable and drive social movements such as Black Lives Matter.

What complicates matters further is that North American and European cities from Toronto to Barcelona have also been unwitting hosts of terrorist activities. In August 2017, fourteen people were killed when a van drove at pedestrians in central Barcelona, and in April 2018, ten people died when a van drove into a crowd waiting at a bus stop. The perpetrators were very different: jihadists and a lone violent misogynist respectively. But the end result was city centres playing host to other expressions of rage and violence.

containment. So, securing neo-liberal globalization is thus rendered dependent on more intense forms of intervention into the lives of citizens around the world. One suggestion is that crime-reducing initiatives like 'broken windows', originally used to justify and legitimate the reform of urban life in 1980s and 1990s

New York, are being used more generally to argue for more
governance, surveillance, and policing. In the original New York
context, the idea was that any form of criminal behaviour needed
to be tackled, such as graffiti. If city authorities failed to tackle the
'little things' then criminals would think that 'bigger things' such
as robbery and violent assault would not be pursued. The 'broken
window' had to be taken seriously.

This analogy is profoundly spatial. There were areas of the city
that needed greater governance including, in the New York
context, the subway. However, the analogy was also powerful
because it highlighted flow and mobility as well. People were
responsible for those 'broken windows' and they had to be tracked
down and prosecuted. Worse still, a failure to act in one area of the
city might encourage other areas to also experience their own
'broken windows'. So 'weak states' and 'thinly governed' territories
even in places like New York are disturbing precisely because they
might act to unsettle and disrupt other areas. From the streets of
New Orleans, in the aftermath of Hurricane Katrina in 2005, to
the alleyways of Baghdad, the juxtaposition of broken windows/
zero tolerance is said to have enabled new kinds of business
and security practices, which Naomi Klein claims empowers
corporations and states to invest, intervene, and regulate through
policing, taxation, and surveillance. Post-invasion Iraq was
rapidly turned into a business-security opportunity for countless
corporations and companies including Halliburton, Bechtel, and
Blackwater. And cities such as New York and London were made
safer and more business friendly, including for tourists and visitors.

Longer term, we appear to be witnessing the hybridization of two
kinds of geopolitical architectures—on the one hand, predicated
on spatial containment, and on the other hand, underpinned by
spatial administration. Neo-liberal globalization, with due
emphasis on market accessibility and privatization, encourages
both variants. President Trump, however, is critical of 'open
borders' and global trade. His vision is more protectionist and

wary of the 'price' that the US pays to support and sustain the international economic and geopolitical order it established in the 1940s and 1950s.

What is likely to emerge in the future is emphasis being placed on spatial administration including state retrenchment and border control. Domestically, as the state retreats increasingly from public sector provision, it is likely to expand in areas such as policing and surveillance. Poor urban communities will bear the brunt of this intervention because it is they who are most likely to be judged to be detrimental to the business of the state. Expressions of 'urban rage' can and do follow as communities feel penalized and marginalized. New technologies and data (e.g. 'big data', automation, and machine-learning techniques) will facilitate further intervention often in the name of more efficient governance. Populations become increasingly surveyed and targeted depending on demographic and socio-economic trending. Externally, it is likely that governments might be more prone to protective nationalisms and closed borders, which will sit uneasily with a world that appears to be on the move or subject to extreme change. Some smaller, low-lying states might be overwhelmed by a rising sea level, while others seek to capitalize on rising demand for resources including food, land, and energy.

Populist architectures?

As neo-liberalism intensifies, despite the protests following the global financial crisis and its impact on citizens around the world, so pressure continues to be exerted on governments and states to reduce their public spending and make themselves ever more attractive and accessible to global investment and business. In the United Kingdom and the United States, for example, this has led to pressure on governments to reduce spending and to encourage citizens to develop more resilient strategies, placing the onus on them to better prepare themselves for further crises and disruption. Within continental Europe there has been an angry reaction from civil society regarding such public sector retrenchment and appeals for citizen resilience. Countries such as Greece, caught up in complex financial restrictions involving European Union institutions, have witnessed widespread protesting and deepening poverty such that the charitable sector has had to step in to fill the gaps left by the retreating state. Compounding such retraction and austerity, regional geopolitical transformation in North Africa and the Middle East has renewed anxieties about uncontrolled flows of migrants that have generated crises in recent years.

What makes all of this more troubling for liberal democracies in Europe and North America is an apparent decline in commitment to the liberal international order. From Donald Trump in the United States to Viktor Orbán in Hungary, political leaders are capitalizing on anger, resentment, and fear about the ability of governments to keep their citizens secure and provide stable employment. Domestic and international geopolitics do intersect with one another, and we have seen plenty of examples of citizens endorsing and resisting populism and even nativism. The liberal international order may be under pressure but there is also a willingness to fight to defend its core values and practices, even if it remains a moot point whether it is equipped to handle a warming world with a population of ten billion. We need to be clear on one thing: the very liberal order that some are worried about in terms of its future health is the same one that many feel has been better at protecting the interests and wishes of the richer and more privileged segments of humanity, often at the expense of other peoples, species, and environments.

Chapter 4
Popular geopolitics

For much of the last decade or so, there has been considerable interest in the popular and visual dimensions of geopolitics and international politics. While the relationship between governments and the entertainment industry is well established in the United States and elsewhere, the intersection can also be awkward. Censorship and repression often goes hand in hand with promotion and support. But whether we focus on satirical comics or popular television programmes, scholars have drawn attention to how geopolitics gets represented and enacted through popular and visual cultures. The distinction between formal, practical, and popular geopolitics is often blurred. When a US president takes to Twitter to announce foreign policy initiatives, for example, it is tricky to determine where the practical and popular begin and end, and how citizens are affected directly by presidential tweets.

Digital media has allowed other actors, including non-governmental organizations, corporations, terror groups, charities, popular movements, and citizens, to occupy the geopolitical spectrum, and produce and circulate their own videos and news stories. Complex geopolitical situations can be narrated and told in 140/280 characters, short videos, and arresting graphics designed to be accessed on smartphones and tablet devices. Popular geopolitics is a great deal more accessible and participatory to anyone who has access to the internet and social media. Within reason, everyone and anyone can contribute and circulate their own popular geopolitics. And there is plenty of opportunity for unscrupulous actors to generate fake users and fake news. It is a complicated mire.

The geopolitical makes itself manifest in the popular cultural realm. Rather than just being representative of the 'real' business of geopolitics, it is more productive to think of this relationship as co-constitutive. So instead of looking at, say, a film about US forces operating in Iraq (e.g. *The Hurt Locker*, directed by Kathryn Bigelow, 2009) and asking whether it offers a realistic portrayal of the conflict, we ask different kinds of questions. How does the action-thriller reinforce or unsettle particular framings of the US-led invasion and occupation of Iraq? Do these artistic interventions help to constitute public understandings of key actors and places, and are they all the more significant when watched and engaged with by audiences that are not likely to have any experience of the places cited? Finally, do popular cultural manifestations such as film, television, social media, video games, books, and so on remind us that geopolitics is fundamentally performance based? Like the generic categories we associate with film and television, are there different kinds of geopolitics based on action-thrillers, dramas, horrors, disaster, romance, and fantasy? President Bush choose to recreate a Reagan-era techno-thriller (*Top Gun*) in May 2003 when he flew a US Navy jet that landed on an aircraft carrier, and then declared that the mission to liberate Iraq was accomplished.

In this chapter, the interconnection between popular culture and geopolitics is emphasized. They are considered inseparable rather than popular culture simply acting as a window on to the real world of geopolitics. As a consequence, my interest is not in whether something is either realistic and/or fantastical. Rather, it is to focus attention on the sensorial nature of popular geopolitics—the power and politics of images and sound. Social media in particular reminds us that images and stories can amplify and exaggerate the controversial and emotive qualities of geopolitics.

Popular mediums such as film and television have, over the decades, been judged to be significant interventions in the making of geopolitical cultures. Television series such as *24* and *The Wire* (but you can add others to the list such as *The Americans*, *Homeland*, and *Battlestar Galactica*) have all been cited as helping to constitute public understandings of the war on terror and cold war legacies, for example. In Scandinavia, so-called 'Nordic noir' has provided examples aplenty of television shows confronting high-level corruption, foreign policy scandals, and geopolitical relationships with NATO and Russia. The Norwegian show, *Occupied* (2015), imagined a Norway in the future being occupied by Russian forces on behalf of the European Union. In the Philippines, the television show *Amo* (2018) provides an uncompromising examination of how the war on drugs is being waged by the government of President Rodrigo Duterte (Figure 8).

8. The television show, *Amo*, which depicts the war on drugs and its effects on the residents of Manila, the Philippines.

What matters is that we also understand those who consume such popular geopolitics as active subjects who are capable of bringing a range of intertextual knowledge and practices to bear on particular media outputs. Norwegians watching *Occupied* might for example feel quite differently about a fictional occupation by Russian forces compared to British viewers of the same show, who might in turn focus on the mendacity of the European Union. Media scholars use terms such as intertextuality to highlight how audiences construct meaning and utilize 'common-sense' understandings of geopolitics and security. One area of particular concern is how far it makes sense to impose any distinction between 'reality' and 'fiction' given the high degree of interaction and interpenetration of what James Der Derian terms the military-industrial-media-entertainment complex (MIME-NET). All of which, he suggests, has led to an ever greater blurring between the civilian and the military, real and simulation, and producers and consumers.

Popular geopolitics and media cultures

Halford Mackinder's focus on popular geopolitics addressed the more formal educational and citizenship structures of states and empires. For Mackinder, material objects such as atlases and globes were deserving of greater scrutiny in late 19th- and early 20th-century Britain. Mass media was of course in its comparative infancy in Mackinder's era compared to today where media is a great deal more widespread, participatory, and digital rather than analogue. Popular communication and media cultures have been radically transformed in the intervening period from post-1945 mass television ownership to a contemporary era characterized by multimedia environments, smart technologies, and greater capacity of citizens to customize their engagements with media such as television, social media, and video. Each of us has our own 'media signature', which is shaped by our access, ownership, production, and interaction with various media objects and organizations including newspapers, radio, television, smartphones, video games, and social media.

Popular culture is creatively diverse, geographically dispersed, commercially varied, and politically multifaceted in nature. It includes the discussion of the production, content, and consumption of Korean pop music, Hollywood film, Japanese animation, British newspapers, Australian fashion magazines, South African advertisements, and Iranian video games. However, the global usage of social media provides another telling example. Nearly two billion people regularly use Facebook but they are overwhelmingly found in Europe, the Americas, and parts of Africa and Oceania. Since Facebook and Twitter are blocked in China, netizens rely on other popular social networks like QZone, QQ, and WeChat, while those in Russia use the platforms VKontakte and Odnoklassniki. Government censorship and control of media organizations in China and Russia as well as Iran and North Korea constrains citizens from accessing Western media sources and digital platforms, thereby limiting the flow of information and culture. Russia and Iran promote their own state TV companies, RT and Press TV respectively.

The production, circulation, and consumption of news and entertainment is inherently uneven and unequal as some agents and communities are better able to produce, circulate, and access different sources. In terms of formal news production, for example, large corporations such as CNN International, Time-Warner, Fox, and the BBC often loom large. They are extremely significant in terms of determining broadcasting content and scheduling, notwithstanding national and international regimes, which can and do exercise some control over audience environments. The newspaper report, the television broadcast, and the internet podcast help determine which people, places, and events are judged to be newsworthy. Such choices then influence viewers' responses, with stories about victims and perpetrators, exploiters and exploited, named individuals and groups, and the nameless. Notwithstanding the exponential expansion of so-called citizen journalism and smartphone technologies (including video-recording facilities armed with email and Twitter-based functionality), media producers such as the BBC are still accorded considerable importance in terms of how their broadcasting material is scrutinized and judged. Media cultures vary greatly from place to place.

But the newer players such as Google, Facebook, Amazon, and Netflix are changing and challenging those traditional media providers alongside digital news providers such as Vox, Salon, and Twitter. Many citizens around the world are accessing news through their newsfeed provided by media platforms such as Facebook, which has two billion users. And if algorithms are shaping those newsfeeds then we might reasonably ask how that affects the type and manner of news being accessed. In a 2017 study by the Pew Research Center, nearly 70 per cent of Americans reported that they used social media to access news. The study suggested that older, less-educated, and non-white Americans were more likely to use social media exclusively for their news gathering. If popular geopolitics is becoming more 'bespoke' and less shared, then does it follow that the popular dimension of geopolitics is potentially more divisive? Many older readers will no doubt recall that in many countries children and adults had access to a limited number of newspapers, and television and radio stations. There was also limited opportunity to publicize and promote your reactions and feedback about particular television programmes and newspaper articles.

The geopolitical power of social and more traditional media, therefore, lies not only in the nature of the broadcasting itself but also the manner in which events, people, and places are framed, selected, and engaged with. It also raises important issues regarding how shared and accessible is information itself in an era where public service broadcasting is less prominent and where it is possible to undermine news and information by manipulating images, monetizing personal data, and circulating fake news. The circulation of images and news broadcasting can also act as a provocation to governments, social movements, and others to demand action. Viewers might have reacted by phoning friends to commiserate, written letters to newspapers, emailed government departments, circulated video imagery, started Facebook campaigns, and composed tweets. In different ways, therefore, the representations of places and people can and do provoke all kinds of emotional investments and demands for political action. Popular geopolitics addresses what gets broadcast and how audiences produce, circulate, and engage with audio-visual materials (Figure 9).

For many in the Middle East and the Islamic world, events such as the civil war in Syria, the Arab Spring, and Israeli–Iranian tension have been animated and magnified by formal and increasingly social media (Box 7). It is now difficult to imagine not witnessing, via social media, citizen journalism of major events such as the overthrow of governments, the exposure of atrocities such as massacres and chemical weapons attacks, and civil conflict. If anything, these kinds of images and sounds have challenged

9. The BBC World Service, Ascension Island, South Atlantic.

Box 7 We love you: YouTube, Israel, and Iran

In March 2012, Israeli peace activists posted a short video on
YouTube featuring a number of Israeli men, women, and children
reassuring Iranians watching the film that they did not 'hate'
Iran. Moreover, many of them were shown to be making the
point that they actively challenged the claims made by the Israeli
government that Iran represented an existential threat to Israel.
With John Lennon's 'Imagine' playing in the background, the
footage of ordinary Israelis professing to 'love' Iran even if they
have never visited the country or met an Iranian was intended to
contest the mainstream geopolitical framing of this neighbour as
threatening. While the audience size in Iran is not known, the
video itself was part of a wider anti-war movement in Israel
contesting the possibility of military strikes against nuclear and
military infrastructure within Iran. A Facebook campaign called
'Israel Loves Iran' was also launched at the same time.

Israel Loves Iran is as much a peace movement as it is a social
media initiative. But it is also an example of public diplomacy
which is not tied to either the Israeli or Iranian governments.
Established by an Israeli graphic designer, Ronny Edry, his initial
posting on Facebook declaring 'Iranians, we love you, we will
never bomb your country', encouraged further campaigning and
inspired an Iran Loves Israel movement (founded by Majid
Nowrouzi). Such initiatives have also encouraged third-party
meetings and video/photographic exchanging, frequently
depicting everyday contexts including family life. Edry and
Nowrouzi later met in person in the United States and there
has been some campaigning to get the pair nominated for the
Nobel Peace Prize.

ideas and understandings of civilian populations who are increasingly willing and able to promote their demands. The French philosopher Jacques Rancière identifies what he calls aesthetic regimes, which determine what sorts of images can be produced and circulated. In Iran, videos of dancing girls (some with their hair uncovered) in the street caused political outrage among conservatives in the country. Accusations abounded that these exhibitions of immodest behaviour were undermining the Islamic Republic of Iran. What might have been considered quite humdrum in the West was judged to be subversive in Iran.

Hollywood and cold war 'national security cinema'

Scholars in cultural history, IR, and political geography explore how the production and circulation of film picks up and engages with ideas and discourses associated with national security and geopolitics. Institutional analyses draw attention to how the film and entertainment industry collaborates with government departments such as the Department of Defense and the US armed forces. For example, why did the US Navy support the making of the 1986 blockbuster *Top Gun* unless they thought it portrayed their activities in a positive light? Those more interested in representations of national security tend to focus on narrative arcs, characterization, place, and dialogue. For scholars working in the field of star studies, another productive avenue of research is to think about how certain actors such as John Wayne, Rock Hudson, and later Clint Eastwood were often cast as strong male leads charged with protecting US national security (e.g. Rock Hudson in *Ice Station Zebra* (1968) and Clint Eastwood in *Firefox* (1982)) or recreating violence and the violent experiences of the US frontier (e.g. John Wayne in *The Searchers* (1956)). And once we do that, we might then ask reasonably what roles did women, people of colour, children, and others play in such films? Did certain actors/characters actively embody the dominant geopolitical imagination of the United States by exhibiting resilience, leadership, and strength?

As America's direct experience of war is more limited, Hollywood generated a whole series of films, labelled 'national security cinema', which outlined in a highly imaginative way threats facing the United States while also instructing viewers about the values and practices the country embodied. The list is a long one and includes Soviet and other communist forces, Nazis, terrorists, extraterrestrials, meteors, uncontrollable natural forces, and machines. Given the widespread popularity of Hollywood productions both inside and outside the United States, it is understandable that films have been viewed as an important contributor to America's visions of its own standing and significance in the world. Defeating enemies helped to reinforce discourses and practices of heroism, military superiority, leadership, and loyalty to the Republic.

During the cold war, most Americans neither encountered a Soviet citizen nor travelled to the Soviet Union. The same could be said for communist China and a host of other regimes of which the United States disapproved. The few that did were likely to be members of the armed forces, the business community, artists, sportsmen and women, and of course spies. For most Americans, Churchill's description of an 'iron curtain' across Europe in 1946 seemed perfectly reasonable, as it did for many Europeans on either side of the Central/Eastern European divide. Film, radio, and later television footage played a crucial role in shaping American impressions of the Soviet Union and the threat posed by communism inside and outside their country. It also helped to consolidate in the main a sense of American self-identity—the land of the free, a beacon of democracy, and a liberal 'way of life' that President Truman had described in 1947.

Film historians have contended that American cold war cinema was at its most important in the 1940s and 1950s. In an era before mass ownership of television, people flocked to the cinema not only to watch films but also to access newsreels and documentaries shown alongside the main feature. What makes these films all the more significant is that Hollywood production companies were closely aligned to various organs of government departments such as the State and Defense Departments and the CIA. In 1948, the Pentagon established a special liaison office as part of the Assistant Secretary of Defense for Public Affairs and the latter was extremely important in shaping storylines and determining whether cooperation would be extended to any production wishing to use American military equipment or personnel. Films such as *The Longest Day* (1961) enjoyed Pentagon support even if some of the US military personnel had to be withdrawn from the film set because of the worsening crisis in Berlin, which culminated with the East Germans building the wall which divided the city until November 1989.

The Pentagon worked closely with producers such as Frank Capra and provided advice, equipment, and personnel for his *Why We Fight* series. The latter was required viewing for all US servicemen and women. This series in particular highlighted the significance attached to visual media by the American authorities in shaping military and public opinion. Given the scale of the threat apparently posed by the Soviet Union, it was not surprising that other agencies such as the US Information Agency and the CIA conceived of film as a vital element in the public campaign to educate American citizens about the dangers posed by the Soviets and to inform others outside the nation as well. The CIA provided secret funding for the animated film, *Animal Farm*, which was released in 1954, precisely because George Orwell's imprint was deemed to be highly appropriate given his allusions to the failed promises of the 1917 Russian Revolution.

During the 1940s and 1950s, Hollywood production companies did not need government funding or interference to persuade them that the Soviet Union and communism more generally posed a danger to the American way of life. America and the Soviet Union had, in this era, clashed over the future of Berlin and the Korean Peninsula. In 1949, the Soviets were confirmed as a nuclear power aided and abetted by the spy Klaus Fuchs. Films such as *My Son John* (1952), *Red Planet Mars* (1952), and *The Thing* (1951) made connections between the threats and dangers facing the American public in this uncertain period. While the first film highlighted the power of communism to influence and undermine the moral compasses of young people, the second and third focused on the dangers posed by aliens to the national security of the country. Taken together, the films seem to suggest that never-ending vigilance was required and that dangerous idealism regarding communism had to be contained.

American political and religious figures such as William Buckley, Billy Graham, and John Foster Dulles also added to this potent discussion and dissection of the Soviet Union and the Red Menace. Graham in particular emphasized the profound differences between the godless Soviet Union and Christian America. Further cementing the popular significance of extremely conservative films like those described above was the political assault unleashed by the House Un-American Activities Committee (HUAC) in the late 1940s and early 1950s. The committee opened its hearings in 1947 and heard submissions from 'friendly witnesses': producers, screenwriters, and actors associated with the motion picture industry. A total of forty-one people were interviewed and a number of other people associated with the industry were accused of holding left-wing views.

Thereafter, the committee concentrated its energies on the so-called 'Hollywood 10'—a group of individuals who refused to answer any questions and claimed that the inquiry violated constitutional protections relating to free expression and speech. The committee disagreed with their stance and all were jailed for their dissent. With the help of the FBI, the Catholic League of Decency, and the American Legion, a list was produced called the 'Red Channels', which contained information about anyone working in Hollywood judged to have a subversive past. Unlike those who appeared before the committee and convinced its members of their innocence, these individuals were blacklisted and effectively denied employment as writers, actors, or producers. Over 300 people including Charlie Chaplin and Orson Wells were listed as having suspect pasts. The impact on Hollywood was considerable and unsurprisingly did not encourage a culture of dissent from the predominantly conservative view of the cold war as a political-religious confrontation between the United States and its enemies.

This of course is not to presume that all producers, film critics, and movie watchers uncritically accepted the geopolitical representations of the Red Menace. Some producers used science fiction and the spectre of aliens to explore radically different interpretations of the cold war zeitgeist. Jack Arnold's *It Came from Outer Space* (1953) featured a group of visiting aliens condemning America's fear of strangers and the unknown. Small-town America is shown to be bigoted and xenophobic in its confrontation with strangers. Stanley Kramer's adaptation of *On the Beach* (1959) depicted the horrors of nuclear annihilation and questioned the strategic logic of nuclear confrontation. Despite government condemnation, the film was one of the highest grossing productions in the year of its release. Another film by Stanley Kramer, *High Noon* (1952), told the tale of a sheriff (Will Kane, played by Gary Cooper) who is refused help by local people even though a gang determined to extract revenge following their earlier arrest threatens his life. For some within Hollywood, the film was immediately seen as a satire on the activities of HUAC and the members of the motion picture industry who colluded with their blacklisting activities.

Between the late 1940s and 1960, the motion picture industry produced well over 4,000 films, with only a fraction genuinely critical of the conservative American understandings of the cold war and geopolitical representations of the Soviet Union and the communist threat. Hollywood, encouraged by the HUAC hearings and later the investigations conducted by Senator Joseph McCarthy, found it easier to produce films that reproduced rather than undermined those implicit understandings of the United States as a country composed of god-fearing, liberty-loving souls determined to resist being seduced by godless Soviets and their extraterrestrial accomplices.

Television and the wars on drugs and terror: the case of serial shows

Television has arguably been the most important popular medium for transmitting information about and engaging with the war on terror. While there have been a slew of films addressing the war on terror, originating out of Hollywood and other cinematic cultures, US-based television shows such as *24, The Wire, Homeland,* and *Battlestar Galactica* have earned popular and critical acclaim for their engagement with terrorism, war, homeland security, and torture. Longer, carefully plotted serial narratives have been used to explore and develop often complex storylines, multiple locations, geopolitical melodramas, and characterization of place (Box 8).

One of the most powerful effects of serial shows is to explore how the domestic and the foreign combine with one another to produce distinct forms of popular and everyday geopolitics. One of the most notable examples has been a number of television shows addressing the so-called war on drugs. First declared by President Richard Nixon in the early 1970s, it has consumed billions of dollars and numerous lives both north and south of the US–Mexican borderlands. The 2017 show *El Chapo*, for example, considers how the drugs trade involves a series of negotiations and concessions within and beyond the Mexican state and cartels and the manner in which US agencies have engineered, manipulated, and profited from the trans-border drugs trade. In the fictional/factional world of *El Chapo*, ordinary people are shown to be caught up in a complex web of relationships including poor farmers, transport workers, illegal migrants, and vulnerable people forced to be traders.

Box 8 Flying the flag: Hollywood, 9/11, and the war on terror

In the aftermath of 9/11, the US media reported a meeting between representatives from the George W. Bush administration and the movie and entertainment industry. Spearheaded by presidential adviser Karl Rove and Jack Valenti, the chair of the Motion Picture Association of America, the idea of the meeting in November 2001 was to explore ways in which popular culture might play a role in promoting homeland security and explaining the declaration of a war on terror. While denying that the administration was asking the entertainment industry to produce movies and television shows 'glorifying' the president, there was interest in exploring how popular media might be used to be 'informative' and 'supportive'.

As a consequence, between 2001 and 2009 (i.e. President Bush's terms of office), there was considerable interest in exploring how popular culture contributed to the construction and diffusion of the war on terror. Cartoons, television shows, films, novels, music, and other outputs including objects such as number plates and souvenirs were investigated. For the critics, they detected a tendency within mainstream media and entertainment productions to reproduce through objects and images a framing that supported the US troops in Afghanistan and Iraq, that ensured the federal government should not be blamed in any way for the 9/11 attacks, and that endorsed the view that the United States was engaged in a global fight against terrorists and terrorism. In short, it is argued that such outputs contributed to and sustained an aggressive form of US nationalism and geopolitics, lionizing the role of the United States and its fighting forces in particular.

Many of these serial shows have also been hugely controversial as well. The award-winning series *24* is an excellent example. Over eight seasons (running between 2001 and 2010), the real-time serial drama follows the exploits of counter-terror officer Jack Bauer and his efforts to ensure the security of high-profile individuals, family members, and entire cities within the United States. The show premiered in November 2001 and enjoyed audience figures running into the millions. Each episode covered one hour only and the show's signature ticking clock was intended to remind audiences of the real-time pressures facing counter-terror officers.

One area of considerable controversy throughout the series was Bauer's use of extraordinary methods such as torture and extreme forms of interrogation. Bauer's modus operandi stimulated a great deal of public discussion at the time and led to fears that this was endorsing the use of extraordinary (and indeed extrajudicial) force in the face of anxieties about terrorism and fears of possible repeat attacks of the scale and size of 9/11. For critics, the producers of *24* were complicit with US government discourses and practices, calling for extraordinary measures to ensure that the United States did not endure a 'second 9/11'. What became apparent following 9/11 was that military and intelligence officials were engaging in similar techniques shown to be the provenance of Jack Bauer. What made the show even more controversial was growing evidence that the FBI and CIA were actively involved in advising and assisting the entertainment industry in its depictions of the war on terror. Chase Brandon, the CIA's representative in Hollywood, was said to be an adviser for the *24* scripts.

But there is another element of *24* that is of relevance to popular geopolitics, namely a focus on what kind of people and places get depicted as threatening or dangerous and by association those that are deemed worthy of protecting and saving. *24*, with its action-thriller qualities, made it an ideal vehicle to project dramatic narratives involving Turkish terrorists and others including Lebanese, Russian, and Serbian protagonists, and some who appear to be determined to unleash terrorist violence against nuclear reactors, shopping malls, workplaces, highways, airports, and suburban neighbourhoods in Los Angeles. What one might take away from Bauer's multifarious exploits is that the sites and spaces of terror are literally everywhere and there are few areas of public life that might not be vulnerable to a terrorist attack: a point made by senior members of the Bush administration who, on introducing the homeland security terror alert system, warned US citizens that they needed to be vigilant everywhere. As President Bush warned the American people in January 2002, 'A terrorist underworld—including groups like Hamas, Hezbollah, Islamic Jihad, Jaish-i-Mohammed—operates in remote jungles and deserts, and hides in the centers of large cities…But some governments will be timid in the face of terror. And make no mistake about it: if they do not act, America will.'

While *24* has been regarded as a neo-conservative endorsement of the need for widespread and ruthless counter-terrorism, it has also informed public critique of the war on terror. Other television shows such as *The Wire* (2002–8), based on the experiences of police officers, criminals, city officials, and others in a poverty-ridden and financially insecure Baltimore, are credited with offering a different view of how the war on drugs, the war on terror, and policing inform one another. The title *The Wire* indicates a central conceit of the show, which was to focus on objects essential to the business of electronic surveillance. Frustrated by their inability to prosecute a major drug-dealing family, the Baltimore police turn to surveillance and exceptional measures, including violence, to disrupt the city's drugs economy. While drugs remain the primary object of concern rather than terror, the series considers how urban America is nonetheless caught in a broader matrix of geopolitical matters including neo-liberal restructuring and security politics.

While located in Baltimore, the political, economic, and cultural challenges facing this multiracial city are not exclusive to north-eastern America but also linked to the fate of other places in the world. Global flows of drug smuggling (the international criminal that supplies the Barksdale family is known as 'The Greek') and corporate/financial investment have left their mark on the physical infrastructure of the city and the residents in multiple sites including public education, media, and local government. *The Wire* suggests that the war on drugs, like the war on terror, is not just an abstract slogan but also indicative of a set of relationships that tie people and places together. In season five, in particular, the show explores how the police and law enforcement agencies carry out the war on drugs, resisted by local residents and framed by media coverage. It is particularly insightful on the impact of certain police-led strategies regarding the drugs trade, insisting that raids and surveillance regimes end up alienating local communities and making it less likely that residents will support attempts to regulate or even eradicate the drugs trade. Some residents are more affected by these anti-drug strategies than others, and in particular the poor and African American communities are depicted as being on the sharp end of the war on drugs. For those charged with waging anti-drug campaigns, the effects are shown to be counterproductive, corrupting, destructive, and disillusioning. Unlike *24*, *The Wire* is arguably a powerful critique of the state of exception (Box 9). It is a cautionary tale of what can happen when the state declares war on an object or an activity. It turns the geopolitical gaze not to external others but to the local, the everyday, and the mundane but powerful consequences of surveillance, raiding, and violence. The primary sites of geopolitics are the streets, the schools, the docks, and the police stations—as dealers and detectives strive to avoid each other.

It asks us to consider the legitimacy and efficacy of violence and whether state-sanctioned violence is any less exceptional and disturbing than the violence of the gangs and criminals. The police and the drug families are shown to be similar—hierarchical, rule-based, irrational, and capable of unpredictable behaviour.

Box 9 States of exception and exceptional states

The state of exception has attracted much attention, and writers such as Carl Schmitt in the 1920s and 1930s explored the relationship between law, politics, sovereignty, and emergencies. Schmitt's interest in the exceptional was predicated on a belief that what made the sovereign powerful was not the regulation of the 'normal' but the implementation of the 'exceptional'. By declaring a state of emergency or imposing martial law, for example, the sovereign ruler or government shows its hand in terms of defining what is permissible and what is not. Films such as *The Siege* (1998) and *Enemy of the State* (1988) offered a glimpse, in a pre-9/11 setting, of how the 'emergency' can be used to claim a necessity for exceptional powers without the normal constraints of law and policing.

More recent authors such as Giorgio Agamben have questioned whether the 'state of exception' is actually that exceptional. In other words, is there evidence to suggest that states are often by default exceptional in their nature, as modern governments claim, and incorporate the powers to defer the rule of law in order to address challenges, particularly those labelled as security challenges? As a consequence, the boundary between law and the exception becomes increasingly blurred as the state normalizes the state of exception itself. Critics of the war on terror argue that practices such as extraordinary rendition, drone attacks, targeted assassinations, mass surveillance, and the like reveal this very exceptionality and increasingly the use of either new laws and/or covert action to circumvent and, increasingly, justify these exceptional practices. Moreover, citizens themselves are also asked to help perpetuate these appeals to exceptionality by spying on one another and reporting wherever possible 'suspicious behaviour'. A more recent film, *The Circle* (2017), addresses how surveillance becomes normalized within a social media company and its employees.

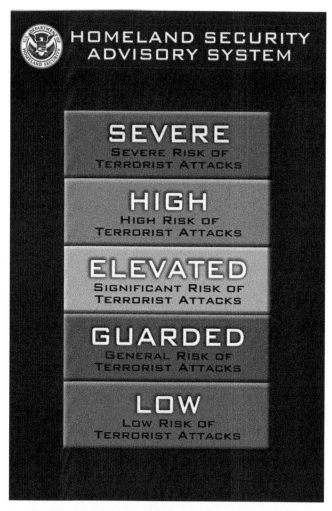

10. The colour-coded threat level advisory system developed for US homeland security: Severe (red), High (Orange), Elevated (yellow), Guarded (blue), and Low (Green).

Both are inhabited by a plethora of 'petty sovereigns' who, in Judith Butler's terms, are (overwhelmingly) men capable of acting in extraordinary ways, which are barely accountable and regulated at times. When posed as a security risk, drugs and terror share commonalities including a penchant for 'working the dark side', 'taking the gloves off', and operating in 'the shadows'. Surveillance ends up neatly encapsulating post-9/11 geopolitics—anticipating, responding, and spying (and making sure that citizens are reminded that the country is monitoring homeland security nearly constantly). Homeland security can and does take on many different hues (Figure 10).

The internet and popular geopolitics 2.0

Since the 1980s, the growth and development of the internet has been widely championed as encouraging further social interaction and shrinking geographical distance. The United States remains by far the biggest user community of the internet and the most significant producer of information. The digital divide between North America, Europe, and East Asia, on the one hand, and sub-Saharan Africa and the Middle East, on the other, is closing quickly. And in the space of two decades, a more participatory form of social media has developed, allowing citizens, corporations, states, and other stakeholders to produce and consume their own geopolitical materials.

Powerful search engines such as Google allow users to access and download images and stories in mere seconds with both positive and negative consequences, ranging from the fear of seditious and offensive material being published on the internet to people being able to access new communities and social networks in a virtual manner. This has clearly allowed all kinds of activities to flourish, including global terror networks and neo-Nazi groupings. Al-Qaeda has used the internet to generate funding, send encoded messages to members, publicize videos of speeches by its leaders, and promote its activities across the world.

Much to the frustration of national governments, the internet is extremely difficult to police and patrol as websites can be shut down but then re-emerge shortly afterwards with a different domain address.

The internet has provided an important medium for the anti-globalization movement and enabled it to challenge both the material power of states, corporations, and institutions associated with the dominant political-economic order and to contest particular visual and textual representations of that dominant architecture. In the case of the first dimension, the anti-globalization movement has publicized and organized global days of action, usually in cities which happen to be hosting meetings of the WTO, IMF, or the G8. More widely, the internet has facilitated the growth and development of social networks such as People's Global Action and the World Social Forum, both of which have enabled activists all over the world to come together to consider alternatives to neo-liberalism and solutions to local issues such as water privatization in South Africa, land ownership in Mexico, and the impact of foreign debt repayments in Latin America.

The internet has therefore allowed individuals and groups committed to protesting about neo-liberalism to exchange experiences, plan action, swap dates, and highlight future events in a way that is clearly far quicker than in the past. The demonstrations organized during a WTO meeting in Seattle during November and December 1999 coincided with what has been called e-mobilization and e-protest. The capacity to circulate images alongside commentaries has also been important in allowing these groups to promote their viewpoints and potentially to shape the news agendas, even though many campaigners complain that mainstream media tends to marginalize their protests and demands for radical reforms of the neo-liberal world economy and its servicing institutions such as the WTO or powerful groupings such as the G8 (Box 10).

Box 10 Global financial revelations

Leaked in 2017, the 'Paradise Papers' revealed a vast array of offshore investments by tens of thousands of high-income individuals and corporations scattered across the world. Eager to avoid personal and corporation taxation, the papers acknowledge the vital role played by offshore financial centres in hiding money from national governments. Cash reserves of large corporations are held offshore and global financial regulation was revealed to be partial and patchy, diminishing the tax base of all countries. This data leak followed the 2015 'Panama Papers' revelations, which emphasized the importance of financial and legal services in providing expert advice regarding tax avoidance and the circumvention of international sanctions. What we might take away from these revelations is how important investigative journalism was in reading and analysing millions of papers, and how the complex geographies of international finance cannot be easily condensed into a 'five-minute read'.

Contesting dominant representations of the prevailing global politico-economic order is another area of activity facilitated by the internet and other media. Corporate television broadcasts of G8 and WTO summits tend, in the opinion of anti-globalization movements, to reinforce rather than challenge the geopolitics of neo-liberalism. Attention is usually focused on heads of states and their delegations as opposed to protestors, who tend to be viewed as a distraction or, increasingly in the aftermath of 9/11, as a security challenge which needs to be contained. As the ownership of the media becomes increasingly concentrated in the hands of larger corporations such as News International, this tendency is likely to increase rather than diminish. As with powerful economies such as the United States and Japan, there is a tendency to support the politico-economic status quo and that includes its accompanying political architecture, which helps to regulate the interaction between territories and flows of people, investment, and trade.

Websites and social media offer alternative news sources (e.g. indymedia.org.uk) and have been used routinely to convey a rather different vision of the world—an unequal one where the richest 10 per cent of the world possess 90 per cent of global income. These sites have also encouraged campaigners to submit news stories and images of global days of action and to submit items about local places and their geographical connections to global processes such as trade, investment, and foreign debt. The Zapatista movement in Mexico and its leadership have pioneered much of this investment in the internet and alternative media, recognizing in the early 1990s that it was a crucial component in their struggles to resist the Mexican state, international financial markets, and the prevailing global economic order. What made their usage so surprising was that internet connectivity was low in southern Mexico. Within two years of launching their counter-offensive against neo-liberalism, the Zapatistas had organized a series of continental and intercontinental meetings in 1996 and 1997 through the use of the internet and email. Thousands attended the meetings and exchanged information with one another, including the American film producer Oliver Stone. The charismatic leader of the Zapatistas (Rafael Sebastián Guillén Vicente also known as Subcomandante Marcos) used the internet to publicize their causes (land dispossession, economic marginalization, and racial discrimination) and encouraged new networks of solidarity in Mexico, Latin America, and beyond. The internet provides a forum for the group to continue their struggle and is also successful in encouraging other groups and individuals to formulate alternative understandings of the global economy, international financial markets, and the Mexican economy. So, in that sense the internet was seen, in some quarters, as enabling and expanding networks of geopolitical solidarity, where there are radical divergences in how money, people, goods, and services are able to cross borders.

As other governments have discovered, however, controlling information posted on the internet can be controversial and difficult, given the efforts of hackers to undermine government-established firewalls—some hacking organizations have explicitly targeted government agencies and corporate web-based accounts in order to expose information security flaws or register such acts as a form of dissent. In the aftermath of 9/11, the US Congress passed the Patriot Act and other legislation such as the 2007 Protect America Act, which enables the executive and key agencies such as the NSA to investigate the internet and email traffic of those suspected of engaging in activities likely to be harmful to the United States. Other states such as Britain have also sought to impose greater surveillance and control over information they consider suspect. The monitoring of individuals and groups, in the name of counter-terrorism, has been extremely significant in terms of governments trying to restore the prevailing geopolitical architecture of sovereign states, borders, surveillance, and national territories.

Since the revelations of Edward Snowden, an NSA employee, in May 2013, public knowledge of mass surveillance (often warrantless spying), and specifically data-mining programmes such as PRISM, have heightened debate about the manner in which internet access and usage is routinely monitored by intelligence agencies including the NSA and CIA. Snowden not only released scores of documents but also revealed how mass surveillance involved international cooperation with other intelligence agencies around the world, telecommunication companies, and internet providers such as Google. When former Vice President Dick Cheney called for 'total information awareness', it was perhaps not apparent at the time how this quest would lead to what some have described as a surveillance-internet-industrial complex. When still a presidential candidate, Senator Obama was critical of the national security state and mass surveillance, but his critical stance softened on assuming presidential office.

More recent revelations about social media companies and personal data serve to remind us how it is not just national security states that collect information on their citizens. What does all of this mean for popular geopolitics? First, we might reflect on how our social media behaviour is not only a security concern for states but also a business/strategic opportunity for corporations and other states. Accusations about Russian interference in the 2016 presidential campaign raised intriguing issues about who, what, how, and where improper influence was being exercised. The popularization of 'fake news' places further demands on how communities and societies have shared interactions. Second, data analytics can be used to shape public opinion in more targeted and personalized ways then previous generations of propaganda might suggest. Third, social media is highly gendered and racialized, with women and people of colour often being subject to the worst abuse. Finally, countries such as Estonia have become digital pioneers in terms of cybersecurity, media literary training, and blockchain technology designed to anticipate and resist digital attacks and denial of service assaults.

Popular and unpopular geopolitics

This chapter has shown how popular geopolitics can be studied with reference to the media and clearly could be extended to consider in greater detail public art, dance, radio, cartoons, and/or music. While established media forms such as newspapers, television, and radio remain highly significant in producing and circulating news about the world, it is new media forms such as the internet and social media practices such as blogging and podcasting that will command increasing attention from those interested in popular geopolitics. As interconnectivity increases, especially in the Middle East, the internet is providing not only an opportunity for viewers to access different news sources but also to articulate their opinions online. In countries and regions where the public sphere is tightly controlled by national governments, bloggers are an increasingly significant presence even if their activities have been subject to harassment, imprisonment, and ongoing surveillance. Iranian bloggers provide fascinating insights into contemporary Iran and offer dissenting opinions with regards to Iran's foreign policy choices, which help explain to interested readers why, for example, many online commentators feel threatened by the military powers of the United States, Israel, Pakistan, India, and China. It is also salutary to think that personal and data surveillance technologies developed in North America and Western Europe have been sold and exported to other parts of the world. So, popular geopolitics in the contemporary era is a paradoxical affair. Unprecedented numbers of people can now log on to digital technologies, generate their own media, and access bespoke information about the world.

But this digital world is also prone to interference and distortion, and is one where citizens and communities end up more polarized and isolated. Popular geopolitics can quickly turn into unpopular geopolitics or populist geopolitics.

Chapter 5
Identities

This chapter grapples with identity politics, because geopolitics is at its heart about imagining and articulating differences between selves and others. How we articulate that difference can take multiple forms, from being playful (Norwegians telling jokes about Danes and Swedes) to being altogether more sinister, such as inflaming intercommunal tensions or stoking homophobia in places such as Indonesia. In Sri Lanka, for example, stories have circulated via social media warning that minority Muslim communities were conspiring against the Sinhala majority. What binds the three together is emotion and what geopolitics scholars call 'affect'. The powerful forces of feeling that shape how we feel about others, some of which may be shaped by shock events such as the 9/11 attacks and/or long-running disputes and expressions of animus. Emotion and affect can also be manipulated; media reporting can inflame, political leaders can and do distort and exaggerate, and publics may be eager to engage with emotions from fear and dread to hope and peace.

Claims to national identity have to be constructed, and historians as well as artists and writers have been at the forefront of noting how national traditions and traits are invented and circulated through public cultures. Historians Eric Hobsbawm and Terence Ranger once spoke of the 'invention of tradition' and made the point that nations are adept at inventing rituals and practices and then claiming that they possess an ancient provenance.

Critical geopolitics is interested in national identities because those 'inventions of traditions' are also grounded and informed by human–place relationships. The making and remaking of national identities is a creative, iterative, and repetitive process. Novels, memorials, and educational materials are inherently geographical because they work with those identity traditions to connect places and territories to cultures and peoples. Identity narratives are not of course restricted simply to the level of the nation state but can and do operate at a variety of geographical scales, from the individual and subnational to the pan-regional and finally to the global. Individuals and objects (Chapter 6) can be at the forefront of the production and circulation of identity politics and self–other relations. Feminist and queer geopolitics and critical race scholars offer powerful insights into how the subjectivity of geopolitics is made and remade, especially via those that are thought to 'belong' to particular places and territories.

Other cultural and political groupings such as subnational groupings, social movements, and diasporas challenge exclusive claims to national identity. As the capacities of states to control their economic, cultural, and political space has been challenged by non-state actors and flows of migrants, asylum seekers, and refugees, so those claims to exclusive national identities have often been made to appear all the more urgent. One example is to be found in Europe via forms of authoritarian nationalism, which are informed by concerns that national cultures and identities are changing. Michael Billig once wrote about banal and hot forms of nationalism, and made the point that national identities and nationalisms have this uncanny ability to appear urgent at certain times and taken for granted at others. Strictures about how national history and geography is taught, when and where comments can be made about public figures, and who belongs to a community or a country vary in their intensity (Box 11).

Box 11 Identity and geopolitics: HMT *Empire Windrush* and the 2014 Immigration Act (UK)

In 1948, the HMT *Empire Windrush* docked in the port of London with a party of Jamaican immigrants. Their arrival ushered in the so-called Windrush generation: British Caribbean subjects invited to the UK to take up employment in areas where there were labour shortages. In 2018, some seventy years after the initial arrival of the *Windrush*, British politics was rocked by a scandal involving the treatment of elderly British Caribbean citizens, some of whom were being deported, declared irregular, and/or denied access to healthcare. After a public outcry, the Conservative government was forced to halt any further deportation of those accused of lacking appropriate documentation. The political scandal revealed the impact of new legislation designed to create a 'hostile environment' for migrants and how British geopolitical visions, which often emphasize the importance of the Commonwealth, can clash with the desire of governments to restrict the mobility of those from Africa, Asia, and the Caribbean. For critics of the government, the 2014 and 2016 Immigration Acts were judged to be institutionally and legally racist in intent and outcome. The border and bordering process clings more tightly to some people than others, resulting in anxiety and fear for those affected.

Geopolitics and national identity

The creation of the modern international political system based on national states with exclusive territorial jurisdictions is commonly dated to 17th-century Europe. Over the ensuing centuries, national governments emerged and were established via diplomacy and international law—a mosaic of states that has now encompassed the earth's surface, with the exception of Antarctica and parts of the oceans. As the apparatus of the state began to envelop the everyday affairs of citizens, national governments—through their control and/or monitoring of national media and/or school-level education—began to concentrate ever greater energy on the creation and maintenance of a national self-identity. As Michel Foucault noted, as part of his interest in bio-political governance, the nation state maps, surveys, measures, and evaluates national populations and territories ever more intensely. In many countries, for example, this is repetitive—we are asked to complete national census forms, register to vote, and submit our details in order to obtain a passport, acquire a social security number, and so on.

In the case of Argentina, for instance, which declared independence from the Spanish Empire in 1810, mapping and surveying was an essential element in national identity formation. The process of creating what Benedict Anderson has called an 'imagined community' took several forms, one of which was the introduction of so-called 'patriotic education' in the late 19th century to generate a national consciousness. The timing of these educational reforms was not accidental; the government of Buenos Aires had not only extended its sovereign authority over a more extensive geographical territory, including the most southerly region of Patagonia, but also had to contend with new waves of immigrants primarily from Italy and Spain who had to be incorporated and inculcated with a sense of what it was to be an Argentine citizen.

One of the most important elements of patriotic education was the geographical lesson that Argentina was an incomplete country. We might even describe it as a geopolitical melodrama: a framing story that political elites turned to when seeking to make sense of certain policies and strategies. Described as the 'Lost Little Sisters', the British annexation of the Falkland Islands in 1833 continues to grate and remains an integral element in expressions of Argentine national identity. School-level education continues to promote this view and ensures that every young school child can draw an outline of the two main islands (East and West Falkland according to English speakers) at primary level. As the reference to 'Lost Little Sisters' suggests, the territory is often described in highly gendered terms: as a sisterly appendage of the body politic, which is continental Argentina (the Fatherland). It is not surprising, therefore, that when the Falklands were 'invaded' by Argentine forces in 1982, the action was vindicated as an act of geographical salvation after an earlier 'rape' by imperial Britain. Remarkably for non-Argentine audiences, crowds gathering in the main square proximate to the so-called Pink House in Buenos Aires cheered the military regime. At the same time, the regime and other military governments in the recent past were torturing and executing their own citizens. Geographical indoctrination seemed so complete that many in the Republic were willing, at that moment, to celebrate this act of territorial annexation.

The British victory in June 1982 did not resolve this territorial crisis. Despite the claims to the contrary by the Thatcher government, Argentine citizens continue to be informed that this territorial grievance remains outstanding. Argentine media organizations and governments encouraged citizens and indeed visitors to imagine this territorial dispute as ongoing. If you open a magazine and examine weather reports for the Republic, the Falklands are labelled as the Islas Malvinas. Since the late 1940s, it has been an offence in Argentina to produce any map of the Republic that did not label the Falklands as Argentine, and for that matter a portion of the Antarctic closest to the South American mainland. Public maps and murals constantly remind the citizen and visitor that the islands are geographically proximate to Patagonia. British sovereignty is constantly condemned not only as reminiscent of earlier episodes of imperialism but also indicative of a particularly distasteful form of geographical overstretch. Since 1982, public war monuments in Buenos Aires and elsewhere provide a further opportunity for geographical and cultural reflection on what they consider should be Argentine national territory.

This apparent obsession with the recovery of the Falkland Islands has broader implications for Argentine national identity. On the one hand, it shaped a view of the Republic as a geographically violated country, which remains highly sensitive to territorial matters, as immediate neighbours such as Chile would attest. Both countries have argued for much of their histories over their Andean territorial boundary. This has sometimes resulted in fraught situations in which both sides argue over remote, unpopulated territorial fragments in areas where ice and rock movements interfere with traditional measures used to ascribe boundary coordinates such as watersheds and mountain ridges. On the other hand, the UK's annexation of the Falklands in the 19th century allowed later government leaders such as President Perón in the 1940s and 1950s to construct a national vision for Argentina as a country eager to dispense with British and other imperial influence. This continues today, as more recent presidents have railed against continued British control of the islands and look upon future oil and gas development with considerable concern. New revenue streams, combined with an increasingly confident Falkland Islands government (which organized a high-profile referendum on its future in March 2013), make it less and less likely that the UK will ever negotiate.

Argentina's territorial obsessions are not unique and similar stories could be told for other countries such as Bolivia, India, and Pakistan, as a result of territorial loss or formal partition. In all these countries, maps are extremely sensitive in terms of what they depict with regards either to national boundaries and/or territorial ownership. Territorial anxieties also help to shape school curricula and broader self-understandings. The national media in that respect can be extremely significant in not only generating a sense of 'imagined community', but also in helping to cement particular self-understandings. In Bolivia, it is common to read, view, and listen to stories about the loss of access to the Pacific Ocean in the 19th century. Successive Bolivian presidents remind citizens of this historic injustice and the importance of the so-called Day of the Sea held every March. The geopolitics of national identity is pronounced in countries such as Argentina and Bolivia because territorial grievances and uncertainties over international boundaries are held to jeopardize claims to national identity and expressions of pride.

In the United States, which expanded its internal frontier westwards, national identity formation has taken on a different expression. If Argentines worry about their territorial portfolio, Americans have been largely preoccupied with the social and racial character of their national community and the security of its southern border with Mexico. The experiences of those such as the Native American, Japanese American, and African American communities stand in sharp contrast to the experiences of white Christian Americans, who continue to shape the prevailing political culture of the country. The political geography of the United States has been profoundly shaped by struggles for other minorities to be recognized by the national polity. The civil rights movements of the 1950s and 1960s and the fight to secure civil liberties for African American communities occurred against the geopolitical backdrop of the cold war. So, while the United States was championing an international liberal order, the 'American dream' was a varied experience for many of its citizens depending on race, class, gender, and location.

At its worse, communities inside the United States were being disenfranchised and disadvantaged by gerrymandering (the deliberate manipulation of electoral constituencies in order to favour some voters over others) and discrimination in housing and jobs. National symbols such as the Statue of Liberty can be interpreted in different ways depending on, for example, individual and community experiences. African American communities located in cities such as New Orleans, in the aftermath of Hurricane Katrina in 2005, made similar politico-geographical connections as it became clear that the federal government had been slow to react to the loss of life and property of the poor and the immobile. African American families were overrepresented in both categories. More recent expressions of urban disorder have attracted critical questions about fairness and equality, led by social movements such as Black Lives Matter and protests over electoral manipulation.

Another contemporary example, following 9/11, would be the apparently ambivalent role occupied by the Arab American and the Asian American communities. Judged by their appearance and skin colour, many Arab Americans and people of South Asian origin have complained of being subjected to harassment, intimidation, and frequent ejections from scheduled flights because other passengers complained about their demeanour and choice of language—Arabic or Urdu rather than English, for instance. As a consequence, the National Council on US–Arab Relations has complained that the community feels victimized and stigmatized because of the actions of fifteen Saudi and four other Arabic-speaking hijackers on 9/11. Far from being inconsequential, this has led to the suggestion that new forms of identity politics prioritize certain expressions of gender, race, and sexuality largely at the expense of ethnic minorities, who are now viewed with fear and loathing, especially if they occupy public and confined spaces such as aircrafts, ships, and trains. It also produces, in contradiction, pushback from some white Americans who resent attacks on 'white privilege' and claims to white domination.

Identity and territory inform one another in the context of nation states. National territories have functioned as seemingly stable platforms for the manufacturing and reproduction of national identities. Institutions such as the national media and education system have provided and continue to provide the capacity to generate particular representations of national communities as territorially incomplete (Argentina), territorially violated (Palestine), territorially aspirant (Palestine, Kosovo, and Kurdistan), and territorially ambitious (China), and as an example to the wider world (the United States) (see Box 12).

Box 12 Facebook and Kosovo

In November 2013, the social network company Facebook decided to list Kosovo as if it was an independent country (following the 2008 Declaration of Independence which is not recognized by Serbia). Prior to that point, Kosovars had to choose 'Serbia' if they wished to establish a Facebook account. It is estimated that some 200,000 users of Facebook transferred from 'Serbia' or possibly 'Albania' to 'Kosovo'. The Kosovo prime minister was apparently told in advance by the social media company of their decision to acknowledge 'Kosovo' as an approved location. Interestingly, members of the Kosovo government were quick to recognize this decision as a positive contribution to Kosovo's public relations and commitment to join the European Union. While Facebook has never claimed to enjoy the power to 'recognize' countries in the way that sovereign states and the United Nations do (and some one hundred countries have already recognized Kosovo as an independent state), it does highlight how the digital diplomacy of states including Kosovo is partly shaped by an interest in the behaviour of social media corporations. It is worth recalling that over one billion people are estimated to be active Facebook users, so this kind of digital recognition of Kosovo will be welcomed by key Kosovo sectors such as government, business, and tourism, although it is unlikely to be welcomed by the Serbian government and those within Kosovo opposed to independence.

Geopolitics and pan-regional identity

National expressions of identity are arguably still the most significant, given the prevailing international political system based on nation states and territorial boundaries. However, identities are not always territorially bounded. Sometimes identities can simply leak beyond territorial boundaries or be deliberately produced so that they transcend the existing mosaic of states and their national boundaries. Europe provides one such example, and the 1957 Treaty of Rome and its antecedents are significant in this regard. Scarred by the experiences of two devastating world wars, European political figures (particularly in France and Germany) such as Jean Monnet and Konrad Adenauer were instrumental in initiating a political, economic, social, and cultural processes designed to promote European cooperation and eventual integration. For West Germany, recovering from the losses imposed by two global conflicts and territorial partition, the Treaty of Rome was not just about promoting European integration, it was also further evidence that the country sought to reimagine itself as an integral part of a democratic Europe and, as it turned out, a geostrategic ally of the United States.

While the experiences of World War II provided the rationale for this project of European integration, the geographical definition of membership was more troubling. Who could join this new economic club? Where did Europe begin and end? Did member countries have to be predominantly Christian in national ethos and outlook? In 1963, Turkey, often described as a geographical bridge between Europe and Asia, first applied to join the European Economic Community and has had a problematic relationship with existing members ever since.

Fifty years later, Turkey's entry into the European Union remains mired in controversy, as some later members such as Austria have articulated fears that this populous country will place considerable economic, political, and cultural strains on the existing membership, and others have drawn attention to the fact that Turkey's commitment to human rights and the protection of ethnic and cultural minorities has been patchy. Lurking beneath debates over labour movement, economic opportunities, human rights, and political integration, critics in Turkey and beyond believe there is a fundamental cultural anxiety concerning the integration of additional Muslims into a Europe that already possesses substantial Muslim communities in France and

Germany. The humanitarian crisis affecting Syria in recent years
has further polarized views about how European societies
accommodate and integrate migrants from the Middle East.
Notably, the current president, Recep Erdoğan, has expressed no
interest in joining the EU, preferring to promote Turkey as an
independent regional superpower.

Historically, geographical representations of Europe have
changed, and it would be fallacious in the extreme to contend that
there are secure understandings of this continental space. Recent
debates over the future of the European Union have frequently
been populated with concerns relating to territory, identity,
prosperity, and sovereignty. In the midst of the Bosnian wars in
the early 1990s, European Union states were berated for being
weak and failing to intervene in an area proximate to the
membership. Bosnian and other European intellectuals poured
scorn on the inability of fellow Europeans to come to the aid of a
multicultural and multi-ethnic country located only two hours
flying time from London and even less from Paris, Bonn, and
Rome. The destruction of cities such as Mostar and Sarajevo in
1992 and the massacre of 7,000 men and boys in Srebrenica in
1995 was interpreted by many observers as a damning indictment
of the failure of this European project to promote values such as
integration, tolerance, peace, and democracy. A quarter of a
century later, European Union members face a situation where
newer members such as Hungary and Poland stand accused of
weakening core values such as the rule of law and the
independence of the judiciary.

These are challenging times. The European Union presents
itself as a champion of liberal democratic values and practices
such as the rule of law, democratic governance, transparency,
accountability, and independent judiciaries. In recent years, this
has been more challenging. One of the most notable examples is
in Poland. In 2017–18, the Polish government found itself in
conflict with the European Commission (EC) over controversial

laws, which provoked an Article 7 disciplinary procedure against Polish proposals for judicial reform. The governing Law and Justice party in Poland outlined a more executive relationship with the judiciary because of the latter's alleged inefficiencies and unaccountability. EC officials contended that the proposed reforms ran against the EU's commitment to an independent judiciary. It is possible that countries can be sanctioned if other member states find that an individual member state is threatening the integrity of the practices and values of the EU.

But the timing of the 'crisis' was awkward. It calls into question the progressive geopolitics that the EU was meant to champion—free movement of peoples, open borders, promotion of trade, international cooperation, and protection of human rights. A combination of financial and migrant crises continues to place considerable pressures on the EU as an open, liberal, and democratic regional project. In the midst of the negotiations relating to a European Constitution, political parties and media outlets debated with some vigour the nature and purpose of the European Union, which now comprised twenty-seven member states (minus the UK, which at the time of writing is set to leave by the end of October 2019). Some political figures on the right wished to see the constitution embody a 'Christian European' ethos and place due emphasis on its geographical identity as a distinct civilization. French and Dutch voters later rejected the proposed constitution and thus effectively derailed its introduction. For non-Christian observers, the notion that Europe could ever be defined as a Christian space would be alarming, given the long-standing presence of Jewish and Muslim communities throughout the continent.

One of the greatest challenges facing many European governments including Britain, France, and the Netherlands is the alienation faced by Muslim communities. One of 9/11 hijackers, Mohammed Atta, was deeply disillusioned with German society while studying in Hamburg. In France, rioting in the suburbs of

Identities

Paris in the summer of 2005 was blamed on the discrimination and racism faced by young Muslim men. Local experiences of alienation coupled with the ongoing crises in Afghanistan, Palestine, Iraq, and Chechnya have contributed to a global sense of grievance. This combination of local, regional, and global religious and geopolitical factors was cited as significant in the motivation of the four men who bombed the London transport system on 7 July 2005.

Such cultural debates over the geographical extent of Europe haunt many narratives of national identity and pan-regional expressions. Turkey's long-standing engagement with the European Union is just one aspect of this predicament, as were the wars that engulfed the former Yugoslavia in the early 1990s. Other areas of pan-European political and cultural life, such as the flow of people both inside the European Union and outside, have frequently provoked anxieties about who is European and who is not. The entry of Poland and Slovakia into the EU led some British newspapers to warn that Britain would be 'swamped' as Eastern Europeans migrated to Britain in search of work opportunities. As with immigration from the so-called New Commonwealth in the 1950s and 1960s, some commentators claimed that the country was on the verge of being overwhelmed by people who were not 'like us'. As with contemporary debates over immigration, references to 'swamping' act as a kind of cultural-geographical code to enact worries about national and even pan-regional identities. For those with a keener sense of history and geography, countries such as Britain have always been shaped by waves of immigrants. The Polish community in the United Kingdom is now one of the largest and numbers around one million.

The membership of the European Union continues to expand, with Bulgaria and Romania joining in January 2007 and Croatia in 2013. While many have been critical of EU institutions and its incapacity to generate an effective sense of purpose and pan-European identity, it is necessary to consider how the EU has encouraged new expressions of national identity. In May 2006, the Republic of Montenegro held a referendum for independence and 55 per cent voted in favour at the expense of continued partnership with Serbia. The role of the EU is particularly interesting because it established the criteria which the Republic of Montenegro should meet in order to have its claims of independence acknowledged. Indeed, the key argument for Montenegrin independence was shaped by a desire to enter the EU, not national independence per se. Many Montenegrins were unhappy that their desire to be part of the EU was being effectively suspended because of the unwillingness of Serbia to surrender suspected war criminals and its previous involvement in violent conflicts involving Kosovo and other parts of the former Yugoslavia. The participation of the EU was without precedent and clearly demonstrates how a pan-European organization can play a decisive role in shaping cultural claims to a European identity.

As with the Baltic countries, such as Estonia, Lithuania, and Latvia, membership of the European Union was seen as an important part of a transformative process which would allow these states to reimagine themselves as 'European' and at the same time less bound up with the affairs and interests of the former Soviet Union. In doing so, the European Union becomes less geographically defined by Western European states and therefore more internally differentiated. But all of this has come under greater stress in more recent years as two issues—economic austerity and immigration control—increasingly dominate relationships not only within the EU but also with proximate regions such as North Africa. In January 2014, Romanian and Bulgarian migrants were allowed to enter other EU labour markets such as the UK, and this provoked a great deal of commentary (once again) about whether the UK was going to be overwhelmed by another wave of East European migrants.

Meanwhile, aspirant countries such as Ukraine are struggling to mitigate an internal schism regarding greater orientation towards the EU on the one hand and Russia on the other hand.

The identity narratives and political practices associated with the European Union have both complemented and challenged those associated with national states. For some the European Union should be considered as a 'Europe of nations', while others seek to encourage a 'United States of Europe'. One way of dealing with these competing geopolitical visions is simply to resolve them geographically; the Euro-zone and the Schengen Agreement provide examples where some states are members and others are not.

The accompanying debates over the geographical extension of Europe are important, as the EU has shown itself willing to extend European Union activities beyond the boundaries of the current membership. In areas such as immigration and anti-terrorism and anti-jihadism, the EU developed an extraterritorial presence in African countries such as Niger. Working with US counterparts, EU countries such as France and the UK have been at the forefront of attempts to seal the border with Libya in order to disrupt smuggling routes for weapons and illegal migration. The investment and involvement by European and US parties has been criticized by non-governmental organizations and local organizations for being inattentive to the local development needs of border communities (Figure 11). In December 2016, the EU signed an agreement with Niger to invest in state-building and infrastructure investment worth some 470 million Euros (around $550 million).

Geopolitics and subnational identity

If regional expressions of identity and purpose complicate the relationship between political entities and expressions of national identity, subnational groupings seeking independence or greater autonomy from a central authority also question any simple

11. EU and Niger representatives (Dimitris Avramopoulos and Mohamed Bazoum respectively) meeting to discuss migration and development assistance, July 2017.

assumptions that identities are territorially bounded. Countries such as Japan and Iceland, which are virtually ethnically homogeneous, have had less experience of subnational groupings challenging territorial legitimacy and associated claims to national identity. Within Europe, communities such as the Catalan community in Spain and the Walloons in Belgium continue to provide reminders that expressions of national unity and purpose are circumscribed and sometimes violently contested by other groupings that resent claims to a national identity or vision.

Nationalism is a dynamic/iterative process and states such as Spain have alternated between trying to repress and accommodate competing demands for particular territorial units and representations of identity therein. Over the last forty years, Spanish governments based in Madrid have granted further autonomy to the Catalan and Basque communities, at the same time as military officials have been quoted as noting that the country would never allow those regions to break away from Spain (Box 13). National

Box 13 Catalonia and the independence referendum of 2017

One of the most controversial moments in Catalan relations with Madrid came in October 2017. Declared illegal by Madrid, the referendum went ahead nonetheless and resulted in an overwhelming number of votes in favour of independence. Turnout was 43 per cent so the nature of the result should be treated with some caution for two reasons: first, some residents choose not to vote because the referendum had been declared illegal by the Spanish Supreme Court; and second, some voters could not register their vote because polling stations were blocked by the regional and national police. The referendum was also declared illegal by the King of Spain, Felipe VI, which added further controversy to the situation. The European Union refused to intervene in support of Catalan leaders, arguing that the matter was an internal matter for Spain. Post-October 2017, pro-independence parties remain dominant in the Catalan regional parliament after the Spanish government used Article 155 of the Spanish Constitution to dissolve parliament in Catalonia and insist upon fresh elections in December 2017. The impasse with Spain's richest region remains.

maps, produced by the National Geographic Institute of Spain (established in 1870), have played an important part in reinforcing visions of a united Spain.

This apparent determination to hold on to those territories has in part provoked groups in the past such as ETA (Basque Homeland and Freedom in English) to pursue terror campaigns that have in the past included bombings and attacks on people and property in the Basque region and major cities such as Madrid. Created in July 1959, it sought to promote Basque nationalism alongside an anti-colonial message which called for the removal of Spain's occupation. The Spanish leader General Franco was a fierce opponent and used paramilitary groups to attempt to crush ETA. This proved unsuccessful, and ETA continued to operate after his death in 1975, notwithstanding various attempts to secure a ceasefire in the 1990s. Most importantly, the group was initially blamed for the Madrid bombing on 11 March 2004, which cost the lives of nearly 200 people (called 11-M in Spain). Islamic militant groups rather than ETA were actually the perpetrators of the Madrid bombings. The then People's Party government, led by Prime Minister José Aznar, who had approved the deployment of Spanish troops to Iraq, was heavily defeated at the national election three days later. Interestingly, a national government haunted by low popularity attempted to blame an organization operating within Spain for a bombing that many believed to be a direct consequence of Spain's willingness to support the war on terror.

While the challenge to the Spanish state posed by subregional nationalisms remains, the use of terror probably receded as a consequence of 11-M. Catalan separatists continue to promote practices and expressions of difference such as languages, regional flags, and maps, and in the case of ETA a geographical space that defines and defends the Basque homeland—Euskal Herria. Not all Basque separatists have supported the activities of ETA in the past, but nowadays the struggle continues through arguments over constitutional powers, financial settlements, and the scope of the Catalan parliament and its leadership to override the constraints imposed by Spanish central government in Madrid. ETA was formally disbanded in May 2018.

For both national states and regional separatists, the struggles to demarcate ownership of territory are considered to be an essential element in enabling particular narratives of identity to be sustained. On the one hand, these struggles in diverse places such as Spain, China, Sri Lanka, or Indonesia help national governments not only to legitimate military and security operations, but frequently to provoke greater levels of financial and emotional investment in narratives of national identity as manifested in popular cultural outlets such as television, schools, and newspapers. The designation of something as a security threat, as scholars of geopolitics and international relations have noted, is often an essential moment in the justification of coercive means as the state is judged to be imperilled. On the other hand, separatist struggles remind us that such claims to national identities should never be taken for granted. The contemporary condition of places like Iraq, Lebanon, and Syria provides a chilling reminder of how colonial borders and multiple identities coexist uneasily, and the imposition of infrastructure and national symbols such as national flags and currencies is barely adequate when there is little local legitimacy and recognition.

Geopolitics and civilizations

Geopolitics

In 1993, the American scholar Samuel Huntington created something of a stir when he published an essay entitled 'The Clash of Civilizations' in the journal *Foreign Affairs*. As with Francis Fukuyama's contribution 'The End of History', a striking title and opportune timing ensured that the essay received considerable publicity both in the United States and elsewhere, including the Middle East and Islamic world. The article set out its store early on. Readers were told that the world was entering into a new phase where a 'clash of civilizations' will prevail in the making global geopolitics. The civilizational clash sat awkwardly with more optimistic readings of post-cold war geopolitics.

Critically, Huntington sketches a new world map populated by seven or possibly eight civilizations, rather than one dominated by a geographical heartland. In Huntington's geopolitical world, the principal threat facing Western civilization is judged to be Islam and its associated territorial presence in the Middle East, North Africa, Central Asia, and Asia. While his understanding of civilization is vague, his depiction of Islamic civilizations as threatening is informed by the published writings of the Middle Eastern and Islamic scholar Bernard Lewis. The latter has been instrumental in informing neo-conservative opinion in the United States, and more than any other scholar arguably helped to inform the intellectual framework of the George W. Bush administration with regard to foreign policy options for the Middle East. Unsurprisingly, other well-known scholars such as the Palestinian American academic Edward Said have been scathing of the work of Huntington and Lewis.

In defining Islamic civilizations as inherently threatening to the United States and the West more generally, an identity politics reminiscent of the cold war continues, albeit under a different cultural-geographical guise. If communism and the Soviet Union were considered global threats for sixty years, Said and others contend that it is now the turn of Islam and regions such as the Middle East and North Africa to be depicted as dangerous and threatening. Even if such an apparent master narrative seems simplistic, Huntington's mental mapping of the world contains some extraordinary silences or omissions. For one thing, the notion that the West is defined as Christian seems to neglect the long-term presence of other faith communities in Europe and North America. Moreover, it is difficult to imagine any civilization that has not been influenced by a whole range of flows including people and their faiths and other socio-cultural practices, including language, food, and architecture. Any visitor to Spain and Portugal would be hard pushed not to notice the continued influence of Islamic architecture and the role of Arabic in determining place names, for example.

More worryingly for Edward Said, in his article entitled 'The Clash of Ignorance' published in October 2001, the idea of a 'clash of civilizations' informs an American world view, which might interpret the 9/11 attacks in distinctly cultural terms. While some Islamic militants might invoke such cultural terms, the inherent danger in such simplistic labelling of places is that interdependence and complexity are sacrificed in favour of monochromatic simplicities. Again, in Bush's America there was no shortage of right-wing commentators such as Ann Coulter who were only too eager to link Christian/Western superiority to a form of American foreign policy which would advocate the unqualified defence of Israel and the destruction of the Islamic world. For the more extreme elements of the Christian evangelical community, the Second Coming of Christ will only be secured once the world encounters Armageddon via a clash with Islamic militants, or more prosaically via global climate change.

Regardless of the source of global destruction, the 'clash of civilizations' debate has highlighted how narratives of identity are also articulated at a global level. These kinds of debates, however, often neglect key elements such as the historical geographies of colonialism. If one wants to understand the ways in which different places and faiths have interacted with one another, then the legacies of cultural, political, and economic dominance and resistance have to be appreciated. The inherent danger of the Huntington thesis is that other places and faith communities are simply represented as threatening. Even if they were, it is striking that commentators such as Huntington and Lewis are unwilling to consider in more detail how the experiences of British and French colonial domination in the Middle East shaped and continues to shape contemporary geopolitical relations. Claims to British or French moral superiority were frequently exposed when those countries subsequently bombed, gassed, and massacred the very populations they sought to order and control.

Egypt in the early 1920s and 1930s was filled with foreign soldiers, and social spaces were segregated in favour of Europeans in a manner later to be replicated in apartheid South Africa. A mounting sense of humiliation and iniquity in Egypt later played a key role in informing the creation of the Muslim Brotherhood and the anti-colonial campaign against the British thereafter. Egyptian radicals such as Sayyid Qutb later visited the United States in 1948 and reported their dislike of its materialistic culture and racial discrimination, especially against the African American community. While there have been a variety of sources and contexts which have inspired contemporary Islamic militancy, the living memories of colonial occupation combined with a dislike of the racist nature of Western liberal democratic states is part of that complex equation. Western powers, with the help of proxy regimes such as Egypt, Saudi Arabia, and Jordan, continued to interfere in the affairs of these states even when they had obtained formal independence. Iranians to this day still highlight the role of the CIA in sponsoring a coup against the reforming Mossadegh government in 1953.

The 'clash of civilizations' promises cultural and geographical simplicities, which frankly don't square well with the complexities of a world filled with interconnected communities and diasporic networks including Christians, Druze, and many Arabic-speaking Muslim communities. Such simplicities might make for comforting reading/listening in some parts of the world but are insufficiently attentive to the complexities of human mobility and accompanying demands that communities might and do make on an array of governments and organizations. Given recent concern over the state of Syria, in the midst of widespread conflict, it is sobering to think that there might be around eighteen million people living outside Syria who have Syrian heritage, including well-known US personalities such as the actress Teri Hatcher and the late Apple boss, Steve Jobs. Prime Minister Trudeau of Canada was one of the most high-profile political leaders who was explicit in his welcome for Syrian refugees arriving in Canada (Figure 12).

Against this geopolitical backdrop, the late Osama bin Laden and his associates presented their struggle as one directed against 'Jews and Crusaders', operating in the Middle East and elsewhere. In his publicized speeches, bin Laden utilized the 'clash of civilizations' to help explain and legitimize the campaign against the United States and its allies, including the apostate regimes of Egypt, Jordan, and Saudi Arabia. His desire to create a new Islamic community (*umma*) was based on the cultural–religious

12. Prime Minister Justin Trudeau welcoming Syrian refugees at Toronto Pearson International Airport in December 2015.

purification of the Middle East and the Islamic world. The ejection of Israelis, apostates, and American forces from the region is judged to be critical in achieving this objective. The latter is most clearly articulated in his 'Declaration of a Jihad against the America's occupying the land of the two holy places', and reiterated again in the aftermath of 9/11. Bin Laden's intellectual world view was shaped by his contact with the Palestinian theologian and founding member of Al-Qaeda, Abdullah Azzam. The latter persuaded bin Laden to travel to Afghanistan, and was an advocate of what he termed 'Jihad and rifle'.

Civilizational clashes have also been imagined within Europe and beyond more generally. Islamic State (IS), operating in Syria and Iraq, mobilizes civilizational discourses, especially those pertaining to a pan-regional Islamic caliphate. Identity politics can jump in scale and location in dramatic ways, from the everyday to the civilizational. Picking up on this turn of events, the controversial novelist Michel Houellebecq's book *Submission*

(2015) imagines France turning into a caliphate, and actively trades on fears of some French citizens that France is losing its traditional Christian character. Open borders and liberal democratic tolerance are blamed for this transformation. In his 2018 book, *The House of Islam*, the writer Ed Husain warns that the relationship between Muslims and non-Muslims remains precarious as migrant flows from the Middle East and South Asia to Europe promote concerns that the latter is losing its Judeo-Christian character. Areas of contention such as the treatment of women, the observance of religious practice, differing fertility levels, and attitudes towards Israel have been used to highlight contentiousness.

President Trump warned European leaders that if they did not respond to migrant flows from Muslim-majority countries then Europe would be changed for the worse. Right-wing parties across Europe warn of the 'Islamization of Europe'. European arms sales to repressive regimes such as Saudi Arabia remind us, however, that civilizational forms of geopolitics reveal contradiction and complicity aplenty. In the meantime, Chinese intellectuals and political leaders have also posited civilizational discourses, arguing that Chinese values and practices are culturally superior to 'Western' geopolitical paradigms because they focus on win–win outcomes, non-interference in the domestic affairs of others, and mutual respect. This has been a crucial element in the geopolitical framing of the Belt and Road Initiative (BRI) as respectful of the identities and interests of others.

Multiple identities, multiple geographies

This chapter has been concerned with the role of identity politics in shaping geopolitical relationships and territories. Classical geopolitical writers such as Rudolf Kjellén distinguished between the territory of the state and the politics of national society, alongside other attributes such as population. But he and others such as Mackinder had less time for social and cultural complexities. The politics of society is inherently more complicated as migration, war, and communicative change have facilitated and forced demographic and cultural change. National storylines, territorial maps, structures of feelings, and appeals to emotion play their part in shaping identity-based geopolitics, but they may include some at the expense of others. The dynamic qualities of identity geopolitics remind us that the geographical relationships individuals and communities have are overlapping and complex. As Michael Billig reminds us, nationalisms and national identities can appear banal when they are simply taken for granted and not questioned. Geopolitics is intimately linked to citizenship and belonging, and the way in which a country/region/civilization understands itself creates policies and practices of inclusion and exclusion.

The way in which the US–Chinese relationship is experienced is complicated and multi-locational, ranging from US students sharing the same lecture space as the daughter of the Chinese president at Harvard to electronic-technological objects and partnerships involving US and Chinese companies. How many American products can you think of that are actually made in China? As with the US–Japanese objects, products, and relations in the 1990s, identity politics can take different expressions and geographical scales; from outpourings of fear and dread to recognition of shared interests and investments. Both the US and China participate in civilizational discourses and practices, as they use their cultural, economic, and political influence in the world to secure advantage and prestige. How those investments and relationships are made sense of will depend greatly on who, what, and where is implicated. The Chinese American novelist, Celeste Ng, captures some of this complexity in her 2014 novel *Everything I Never Told You*. In her fictional world, 1970s cold war America, a Chinese American family are forced to deal with bereavement, racism, and enduring suspicion of immigrant outsiders.

Geopolitics

Chapter 6
Objects

Geopolitics is more than words and images. This final chapter explores the role of objects, and what the anthropologist Daniel Miller terms 'stuff'. Geopolitics is often imagined through objects, but it is also exercised with objects. If you Google image 'geopolitics', the images show maps, globes, notable buildings, military equipment, national infrastructure, and the like. Maps act not only as a way of seeing the world, but they are also physical objects found in atlases as well as applications to be downloaded onto smartphones. Some of the most dramatic moments of geopolitics have involved political leaders looking and pointing at maps.

The role of the object in geopolitics is not always dramatic, therefore. Sometimes objects can be banal and 'hot' (Figure 13). Sometimes they can be militarized and sometimes mundane. Michael Billig's apt phrase 'banal nationalism' highlighted well how things like flags can be part of a wider repertoire of taken-for-granted national expression. Suddenly, however, when they are ripped down and burnt by angry crowds protesting about the foreign policy behaviour of a particular state it can take on a very different standing. Arch-rivals Greece and Turkey have removed rival flags from a disputed islet in the Fournoi archipelago, a strategically sensitive area of the Aegean Sea where eastern Greek islands lie close to the Turkish coastline. Greece and Turkey repeatedly accuse each other of violating

13. Kurdish protestors taking down a Turkish flag inside an air force base in June 2014.

their respective airspace and territorial sea. The flag-planting rivalry matters because Turkey contends, to Greek consternation, that the islet lies in what they term 'grey zones' of uncertain sovereignty. Both sides have been swift to accuse each other of revanchist geopolitics—a desire to reverse earlier territorial losses. Objects of territorial ownership like maps and flags are central to the dispute.

Objects can shape geopolitical relations and illuminate state authority. So, the flag is a powerful, and hyper-visible, expression of state security while at other times it is barely noticed in everyday life. Objects play a key role in securitizing, regularizing, and disciplining our lives. When flags appear out of place—we tend to notice their presence when they are destroyed, taken down, burnt, and torn up—moods can and do change quickly. While we may choose to ignore such things, objects have a way of slipping in and out of our attention spans. Whether we choose to neglect them, play with them, accept them, and/or break them, they help to bring the human and non-human elements of geopolitics into contact with one another—without assuming that objects do not enjoy their own agency to enable, disable, and transform human practices. For example, strong winds and extreme weather can reduce flags to tatters without the need for any human intervention.

The focus on objects is intended to extend our discussion of geopolitics from the earliest observations by scholars such as Halford Mackinder, who spoke about the importance of objects such as railways, ships, telegraphs, furs, timber, coal, and other objects deemed necessary for state and imperial power. For Mackinder these objects were either resources or infrastructure which were largely under the control of human agents. Environmental factors could frustrate their usage, such as ships attempting to cross through an icy sea, but there was less attention given to the role of objects in fertilizing geopolitical imaginations and practices. So how do objects such as the atomic bomb contribute to expressions of American and Soviet geopolitical power (Box 14)? The focus of more recent critical forms of geopolitics has been to consider how objects help to constitute the geopolitical in ways that might also exceed the capacity of humans to control them. And are there objects that might not have been considered geopolitical by earlier iterations of geopolitics that are unquestionably integral to the subject? As a consequence, the chapter deliberately considers counter-intuitive examples such as toys and trash.

Box 14 The atomic bomb and the cold war

Can there be anything more iconic than the atomic bomb and images of the mushroom cloud? First dropped on Japan in August 1945, the emergence of the Soviet Union as a nuclear weapon state was a strategic game changer in 1950. The bomb, as it was often termed, became normalized within cold war cultures: something to be photographed, filmed, written about, and spoken of. In other areas of the world, such as the Marshall Islands, the bomb had a very material presence. After World War II, Bikini Atoll was handpicked to be a nuclear test site. Between 1946 and 1958, the US Air Force dropped sixty-seven bombs, which led to population displacement and long-term poisoning. It is photographs from some of the Bikini Atoll testing that bequeathed us those enduring images of the mushroom cloud post-detonation. Materially, atomic bombs when not exploded were archived, stored, and exhibited in a variety of settings from military parades to museums and public exhibitions. Visitors to Arizona, for example, can visit the Titan Missile Museum with its promise to 'uncover the secrets of America's largest nuclear weapon'. Between 1963 and 1987, the Titan II missile was tasked with guarding the US homeland from possible Soviet attack. Visitors can immerse themselves in the control and command centre and recreate the launch sequence—something that is playful and counterfactual. Thankfully, those missiles were never fired.

Pipelines

Let us start with an object, or series of objects, that are often held to be emblematic of energy security and resource geopolitics: the pipeline. As an object, albeit a highly complex one, involving pump stations, feeder pipelines, and terminals, it has been enormously productive of geopolitics. Supported by expert knowledge, instruments and data flows, modelling and monitoring, and repair and maintenance, the pipeline is part of a wider infrastructure network.

The Trans-Alaska Pipeline (TAP), built in the mid-1970s, is one of the longest pipeline systems in the world, stretching from Prudhoe Bay in the north of the state of Alaska to the port of Valdez in the south. Built in the aftermath of the 1973 oil crisis, it was intended as a dramatic response to anxieties that American energy security was increasingly beholden to a small group of oil-producing countries in the Middle East and elsewhere, such as Nigeria and Venezuela. The sharp rise in oil price transformed the discovered and undiscovered potential of the Prudhoe Bay oil field, where petroleum resources had been found in the late 1960s.

The construction of the pipeline was hugely challenging, as the immense metal structure needed to be able to withstand extreme weather and hundreds of miles of challenging and changeable Arctic landscapes. The flow of oil began in 1977, and since the late 1970s the TAP has facilitated the shipping of over fifteen billion barrels of oil. The production and circulation of oil transformed the Alaskan economy and the parameters of the US energy security debates. But it was also deeply controversial and divisive. So, while the TAP was a response to global energy shifts, the pipeline itself as an object was a source of discord. For conservationists, the TAP was emblematic of a 'rush to oil' regardless of the cumulative impact of a large construction project, which was operating in an environment subject to climatic extremes.

For native populations, the pipeline project appeared to be not only indifferent to the consequences of placing a large object over vast swathes of the Alaskan landscape but also inattentive to revenue sharing. Who would benefit from the flow of oil from northern Alaska to the south, and would it be only the 'Lower 48' states? In October 1971, President Nixon agreed to the Alaska Native Claims Settlement Act, which stipulated that if native Alaskans renounced their land claims in the areas affected by the pipeline project then the US government would transfer $900 million and 148 million acres of federal land in compensation. The provisions of the Settlement Act were distributed among the communities concerned and, as a consequence, the TAP project was completed.

The TAP pipeline was not only productive of global energy geopolitics but also indigenous geopolitics, which brought to the fore how indigenous communities were treated by federal/state-level governments. Since its entry into the union in 1959, the state of Alaska was depicted as both a resource frontier but also a highly militarized space, at the front line in terms of cold war antagonism with the Soviet Union. Less concern, however, was expressed for indigenous and northern communities, who were more likely to be considered 'obstacles' to security and development. The pipeline, in its various manifestations, transformed the geopolitics of Alaska and altered profoundly the manner in which this territory and its infrastructure was imagined and managed.

But the pipeline system, as a complex object, can also produce different kinds of geopolitical relations and geopolitical melodramas. In the winter of 2006–7, European media outlets were releasing multiple stories about Russian gas supplies and the role of Ukraine as a pivotal state lying betwixt Russia as supplier and Western Europe as market. The disruption of supply, prompted by an argument between Ukraine and Russia over gas prices and lack of payment on the part of Ukraine, led to speculation that gas supplies would be disrupted and Western European homes would be starved of heating. Russia accused Ukraine of 'stealing' $25 million worth of gas exports destined for European customers, and other countries such as Moldova complained of being 'cut off' because they failed to pay the price charged by the Russian supplier, Gazprom. Maps of European gas pipelines further reinforced the geopolitical power of the pipeline itself and the capacity of Russian gas producers to alter or even stop the flow of gas. The mobility of gas, as enabled by the pipeline, appeared in peril. Transit countries, such as Ukraine and Belarus, were reimagined as strategically significant precisely because supplies of gas had to pass through pipeline infrastructure located within their national territories.

For some commentators, the 'gas war' was indicative of a resurgent Russia, eager to remind the world that it was an 'energy superpower', with the pipeline enrolled as 'evidence' of such a proposition. Without gas, the pipeline's promise of regular supply to European markets was dashed. China's BRI is a good example of how pipelines can facilitate diplomatic exchanges and are linked to further infrastructural and financial investment packages, some of which may be funded by the Beijing-based Asian Infrastructure Investment Bank.

Objects such as pipelines can be a panoply of identity-based geopolitics. In the case of Europe and Russia, the latter supplies some 25 per cent of natural gas to its Western neighbours, and the dominance of Russian gas in national energy mixes is higher the closer one is to Moscow. The most dependent countries are the Baltic States and former Warsaw Pact countries such as Bulgaria and Romania. Further west, countries such as the UK are served by Norwegian gas supplies. There are a number of pipeline networks such as Nord Stream, Yamal, and Blue Stream. There is also a South Stream pipeline in development, which would allow a fourth route for Russian gas to travel to European Union customers and others such as Belarus and Ukraine. Rival networks such as the Trans-Adriatic pipeline are smaller and allow another gas supplier, Azerbaijan, access to southern European markets.

Russia's pipeline dominance might, in the longer term, be disrupted by the investment in liquefied natural gas terminals across Europe and EU determination to break the overreliance on Russian energy through anti-competitive measures. Eastern European countries such as Poland have embraced shale gas extraction as part of their determination to reduce dependency on Russian natural gas supplies.

Maps

At times of war and international discord, it is perhaps not surprising that public interest in maps and the places they represent is greatest. The power of the map lies not just in its ability to represent places and peoples in multiple ways, but to be understood in a variety of ways as well. As Benedict Anderson noted, the map (and manifestations such as the British imperial map, which depicted colonies and territories as either red or pink in colour) was instrumental in shaping generations of citizens, and how they divided the world up into distinct places and zones. In the cold war period, the development of the North Pole-centred azimuthal projections were credited with introducing American citizens to a new way of looking at the world, one in which the relative geographical proximity of the Soviet Union, via the Arctic, was emphasized. More generally, such projections were credited with shaping a new 'air-age', where the flight path of the plane reshaped a sense of distance and geographical relationship with other countries and continents.

As an object, the map can be pointed at, torn up, altered, hidden, and generally put to work in cementing and contesting state power. Taking multiple formats, digital and non-digital, maps play an important role in the making of geopolitics, which exceeds their practical value in terms of locating places and helping users navigate more generally. Domestically, states have used modern mapping techniques (as part of the bio-political governance noted in Chapter 5) to harvest data on citizens and their movements via private and public transport, to construct maps of urban risk, and to plan future development of cities and infrastructure. Corporations collect sales data and social media companies harvest personal data in order to better understand consumer preferences and habits. Digital mapping is intrinsic to the way in which the state and corporations exercise cartographic power.

At the edge of national territories, the map has been central to the mediation of states and the international system, especially when it comes to the delimitation of borders. Other objects such as stones, trees, signposts, and barbed wire were essential elements in the articulation of borders, as well as features such as rivers and mountain ranges. With the development of scientific cartography from the 16th century onwards, the production of maps was increasingly significant in outlining the boundaries of states and their existence helped to facilitate subsequent endeavours to mark and secure borders. This process continues apace in the maritime domain with coastal states investing large sums of money to map and chart their outer continental shelves in the expectation that sovereign authority can be extended over the seabed (with the promise of greater access to resources lying on or below the ocean floor).

The map can also be tremendously productive of contemporary geopolitics. A striking example is a new national map, with a pronounced vertical dimension. Produced by Sino Maps Press, a cartographic body under the control of the Chinese State Bureau of Surveying and Mapping, the map was released in September 2013. What was notable about it was the capacity of its existence to generate unease among neighbouring South East Asian states on the one hand, and Arctic states on the other hand.

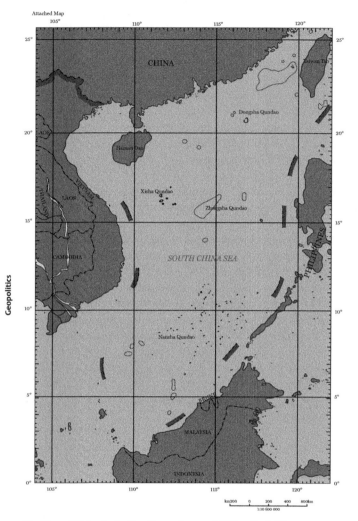

Attached Map

14. **Map of China including the controversial Nine-Dash Line.**

What caused concern in South East Asia was the introduction of the so-called Nine-Dash Line on to the map itself, implying that China enjoyed strategic interest across the South China Sea. The first nine dashes cover the South China Sea while the tenth dash envelopes Taiwan. The latest Chinese passports have this map embedded in them, and of course every time Chinese citizens travel overseas the map travels with them (Figure 14). The point of the map is declaratory—China has substantial territorial and resource interests and rights and it is not going to give them up.

The South China Sea is a deeply contested maritime region. A number of islands are disputed and as a consequence so too are claims to maritime authority in the form of territorial seas, exclusive economic zones, and even sovereign rights to the extended continental shelf. China is locked into a conflict involving the Philippines, Vietnam, Brunei, Indonesia, and Malaysia as well as a long-standing dispute with Japan over the islands of Senkaku/Diaoyu further north. The appearance of the dash would seem to suggest that China considers its sovereign authority to extend virtually all over the South China Sea. While the map acknowledges that the 'boundary [is] not defined', this map has become, quite literally, an object of discord.

The ambiguity of the 'dash' on the map contributes, it is argued, to regional anxieties about the present and indeed future intent of China and its projection of maritime sovereignty. Likewise, the vertical projection of the 2013 map emphasizes China's relative geographical proximity to the Arctic region. In May 2013 China was admitted as an observer to the intergovernmental forum, the Arctic Circle, and it officially describes itself as a 'near-Arctic state'. Arctic states such as Canada and Russia worry about the long-term intentions of China in the Arctic.

Finally, the map as an object can become the subject of counter-geopolitics and counter-mapping. So far we have talked about fairly conventional maps and map making, as tied to the state and its geographical imagination. The experimental geographer Trevor Paglen has been a notable example using new cartographic technologies and applications (e.g. Google Earth) and visual methodologies to generate different kinds of mappings. Since the onset of the war on terror in 2001, Paglen has revealed other invisible objects too, such as CIA extraordinary rendition flights and an accompanying network of destinations and stop-off points including Jordan, Ireland, Qatar, Libya, Afghanistan, and Guantánamo Bay (Cuba). Working with artists and curators, his publications, including *An Atlas of Radical Cartography*, considers a number of maps including images of US oil consumption, and European Union detention patterns regarding illegal migrants.

The term radical cartography, or indeed counter-cartography, is intended therefore to do two things: first, to highlight what conventional maps (often preoccupied with state territories and international/domestic boundaries/jurisdictions) simply miss or under-emphasize; second, to challenge, politically and geographically speaking, phenomena and relationships that might not be considered worthy of being mapped. So, while we can imagine why US government authorities might have been reluctant to produce official maps showing the flight paths of extraordinary rendition-related planes, we might also wonder why other maps are never drawn in the first place. When North American and European governments express anxiety about illegal migration, we might juxtapose the actual numbers of such migrants with the kinds of figures having to be handled by other states like Pakistan and Jordan in the aftermath of civil war, disaster, and the like. Such maps may make use of data sources that are ignored or marginalized in mainstream geopolitical debate.

As maps are increasingly thought of as being the products of geographical information systems rather than hand-drawn by a coterie of skilled artists/technicians, so the map as a digital tool is potentially more widely available than ever before. Artists, as well as citizens more generally, are developing their own maps, and these virtual objects are interacting with the material world. Maps, however, continue to be powerful precisely because they can highlight some things at the expense of others, and the work of Paglen and others is about challenging the notion that the map is an object or manifestation of state power. Citizen mapping is proving highly influential in challenging state-sanctioned maps and data analysis. So, what is significant is not just the representational qualities of the digital map (in other words, the actual content), but also that it mimics the material qualities of official maps—with legends, scales, and so on. The widespread availability of mapping software and open-source data has radically changed the ability of citizens and non-state actors to produce their own cartography and challenge the state dominance of map making. In 2013, for example, Dronestagram (dronestagr.am) was established, and allows users to share drone imagery, including geo-referenced materials. Such photo-, video-, and image-sharing sites provide further opportunities to map and counter-map national and international territories, and challenge the traditional mapping monopolies enjoyed by states.

Trash

What might trash tell us about geopolitics? For those working on the borderlands of the United States and Mexico, material objects such as water bottles, shoes, medicines, and identity documents help to create an intimate introduction to the desperation of those who seek to cross semi-arid environments in a frantic attempt to enter the United States. For a number of writers, including geographers and political scientists, the trash itself becomes a way of thinking about how the environmental circumstances surrounding the borderlands are integral to understanding border protection and regulation. Since the mid-1990s, there has been a deliberate strategy on the part of the US government to shift illegal border traffic to more inaccessible and hostile parts of the border, in particular where mountains and deserts predominate.

As a consequence of these 'natural barriers', the pathways of illegal migrants are more likely to involve traversing wildlife refuges and national parks, which has had implications not only for the survivability of migrants but also for the impact of migration on ecosystems. For those who work on and study the borderlands, there is a greater array of objects and materials to be found either discarded or simply lost by those seeking to cross over. On the one hand, the presence of the trash has encouraged citizen groups to arrange cleaning-up operations; on the other hand, human rights activists have pointed to the presence of discarded water bottles to make the case that ever greater numbers of migrants are perishing due to dehydration in these unforgiving environments, pointing to what they argue is the outcome of those very border security strategies, which were designed to deter (or worse encourage a higher human toll by the strengthening of border infrastructure closer to well-known border-crossing points). So, these objects become a way of documenting and recording the by-products of illegal migration and border security practices. Recent memoirs by border patrol officers such as Francisco Cantú have added further poignancy to finding trash alongside the decaying remains of those who tried to cross the border. In *The Line Becomes a River* (2018), Cantú does not spare the reader the tragic consequences and complicities of border geopolitics and associated immigration controls.

But waste can intervene in other ways and be productive of geopolitics. What might the dumping of waste tell us about how places and communities are inserted into circuits of power? One notorious example involves the Dutch company Trafigura, which was accused of offloading some highly toxic waste in the African country of Ivory Coast in 2006. A local dumping company was subsequently accused of illegally disposing of the waste rather than processing it safely. The controversy intensified as reports unfolded of death and illness being attributable to the illegal dumping. Trafigura was forced to pay compensation to the Ivory Coast government. What transformed this case into something more notorious was a long-drawn-out legal conflict involving attempts to impose a super-injunction preventing news media organizations reporting on the toxic waste dumping, and contesting claims that the incident revealed corporate malfeasance and human rights abuses. What provided a further element of controversy was the geography of disposal. The opportunistic choice of a West African state raised the spectre that this was a deliberate attempt to ensure that European populations were not directly affected, and a cynical strategy to avoid higher waste-processing costs in a country such as the Netherlands. The health risk posed by this form of waste was being outsourced elsewhere. In November 2012, the company agreed a settlement with the Dutch authorities entailing a fine and compensation package.

The geopolitics of waste is often indicative of a transnational, multidimensional, and uneven activity involving production, transportation, disposal, and recycling. As the Trafigura scandal demonstrated, multiple actors were involved including companies, communities, governments, media, and non-governmental organizations. But sometimes 'waste' and 'trash' can offer opportunities as well. One only has to think of benign examples when cargo, often in the form of containers, falls away (by accident or design) from ships, planes, and trucks and ends up in accessible areas such as beaches, encouraging local communities to take opportunities to 'recover' objects from those containers. Accidental waste, in the case of the shipping accident, becomes an opportunity for others to benefit from such flotsam and jetsam.

A more sinister example would be the nuclear fallout and waste associated with the Chernobyl disaster of April 1986, when a nuclear reactor exploded at a power plant in Ukraine. In the disastrous aftermath, Ukrainian nationalists mobilized resentment and anger against Russian/Soviet elites in Moscow for their poor management and maintenance. The disaster became a lightning rod for expressions of Ukrainian eco-nationalism and Soviet-era incompetence.

Waste geopolitics is not just an earthly matter either. While there are atmospheric wastes, such as pollutants held responsible for thinning the ozone layer, there is also space debris. In the mid-1990s, an intergovernmental space debris coordination committee was established involving the major players (e.g. Europe, United States, China, India, Japan, and Russia), but the recommendations of the committee are voluntary. Space trash had raised the possibility of space collision, and there is growing investment in space surveillance programmes in order to enhance national capabilities to monitor and track debris movements. Collisions do occur, however, and in February 2009 a pair of Russian and US satellites hit one another. Due to the extreme sensitivity of their satellite operations, the two countries do not share or coordinate data. EU attempts to promote a Code of Conduct for Outer Space Activities (promoted since 2010) remains mired in disagreement. While most parties accept that space debris is an issue, there is a concern that China, Russia, and the United States appear unable to agree on how to address the problem of space trash and whether any measures designed to mitigate should be binding. This might change, of course, if the debris proves more disruptive of existing satellite operations. Further collisions might then hasten interest in implementing a more binding agreement on space debris.

Action toys

Recent work in critical geopolitics has addressed a field called 'ludic geopolitics', with due emphasis given to toys and connections to playful practices. Toys have had a long-standing relationship to militarism and warfare. They have been, and continue to be, used in recruitment drives, equipment design and testing, and as objects designed to legitimate and justify military behaviour. In the cold war era, rocket and tank toys made by toy manufacturers such as Dinky were designed to inculcate the young citizen with a scaled-down version of those weapon systems which were located in various locations around the globe.

As children's play scholars showed, military-themed toys helped to render weapons of mass destruction understandable to a generation of children growing up at the height of the cold war, including the 'space race'.

For my generation, born in the mid to late 1960s, the introduction of the action figure looms large, especially for young boys (but not exclusively). In the United States, Hasbro launched GI Joe in 1964 and within two years the UK toy manufacturer Palitoy introduced Action Man. In both cases, this toy soldier was radically different from earlier iterations of the metal figure. Designed as a mannequin doll, it was, as Tara Woodyer's research suggests, a risky business venture. Previously such dolls were associated with girls and their play-based behaviour, especially Mattel's hugely popular Barbie doll. The GI Joe range was marketed as 'action' figures in order to distinguish them from the more 'passive' Barbie dolls. The design of the 'action man' was deliberate in the sense of being highly flexible and capable of being dressed and equipped in multiple iterations. For a young boy growing up in Britain in the 1970s, my Action Man came with fuzzy hair and scarred facial skin and was equipped with hands that were able to grip a growing arsenal of weapons and assorted equipment. With a choice of clothing and vehicles, my brother and I were able to invent ever more elaborate warfare and adventure scenarios in our bedrooms (in winter) and in the garden (in the summer). Our Action Man dolls survive to this day, albeit stored away in the attic of my house. What is striking, looking back at that period, is how the enemy forces were imagined to be more reminiscent of German forces in the 1940s rather than Soviet/ Warsaw Pact adversaries armed with their distinctive AK-47 weapons (Box 15).

What is interesting about the development of the Action Man figures is that its design and consumer popularity enjoyed a changeable history. There was no 'Action Woman', and the equipment and uniforms were based on the UK armed forces.

Box 15 The AK-47 machine gun

If there is one gun that typifies the importance of the armed weapon as a material object in geopolitics, then the AK-47 assault rifle would be a prime contender. Developed in 1945–6 by the designer Mikhail Kalashnikov, this gun not only became the official rifle of the Soviet and Warsaw Pact forces but was widely circulated and distributed in other parts of the world. Cheap to manufacture, light to carry (and thus a weapon capable of being used by children), and easy to maintain, it was the weapon of choice of countless armed forces, criminal gangs, and revolutionary movements. The gun was smuggled across borders on an industrial scale, and the design widely copied by other manufacturers including China and Israel. The AK-47, symbolically, was adopted on the flag of non-state actors such as Hezbollah and on the coat of arms of states such as Burkino Faso (1984–97).

All my Action Man figures were white, but it was possible to buy a black Action Man called Commando Tom Stone in the 1970s. Members of the British military were invited by the toy manufacturers to advise on the design of the dolls. There were variations within Western Europe. The German equivalent, during the cold war years, was less overtly militarized, and equivalent figures were dressed in UN peacekeeping materials. In the United States, GI Joe became less popular during the Vietnam conflict, and it was not until the emergence of Ronald Reagan as president in the 1980s that the brand was relaunched as a 'Real American Hero'.

The ebb and flow of cold war geopolitical tension played a part in the emergence and circulation of these particular toys. The Action Man brand was relaunched and rebranded in 1993–4, but more as an action adventure figure than a military doll. Action Man returned to its military roots in the midst of the VE (Victory in Europe) Day commemorations in 2009. Licensed by the Ministry of Defence in the UK, the HM Armed Forces range involves the active cooperation and engagement of military personnel in the design and promotion of war toys. The marketing for these toys stresses a high level of realism in terms of clothing and equipment design. It was actively promoted in children's magazines and via television adverts during widespread coverage of UK military operations in Afghanistan and Iraq between 2001 and 2015.

The commercial popularity of the HM Armed Forces range is partly due to the design quality of the dolls (as noted by multiple reviewers on internet forums), but is also indicative of what might be thought of as a re-enchantment with the British military forces. While not shared by all UK citizens, there has been an upsurge of 'support the troops' initiatives, including homecoming parades, 'Help the Heroes' charitable giving, commemorative ceremonies, and other activities including popular music events designed to highlight the contribution made by UK military personnel in Afghanistan in particular. Play with toys such as the HM Armed Forces action figures becomes all the more interesting for its contribution, among many other objects such as arm bands, in domesticating and normalizing military activities and militarism more generally. But these toys can also become objects of protest and dissent, so it is important to note that the relationship between toys, militarism, and geopolitical cultures is never straightforward.

Objectifying geopolitics

This chapter on objects and material culture more generally is a recognition that geopolitics is fundamentally about stuff and what we do with it. While we might think of the more formal architecture of the state such as maps, monuments, and mementos, there is no shortage of examples that help us think with objects (Figure 15). Objects get put to work in a variety of ways. They can be disobedient and thus capable of encouraging, frustrating, and even resisting

15. The Monument to the Fallen in the Malvinas/Falklands, Ushuaia, Argentina.

human agency. The flag does tear, the gun does jam, the licensing device does fail to record, the Action Man does fall apart from childish abuse, and the container gets used to transport prisoners in Afghanistan rather than trade goods around the world. Part of the challenge posed by objects to geopolitics is that there are so many things one might consider, and there are examples which can suddenly become 'geopolitical' when previously they might have been considered marginal, insignificant, and/or banal. Finding micro-plastics in the central Arctic Ocean can become a 'call to arms' for many, and lead to the reimagination of remote spaces as areas of pressing concern.

Objects and the corresponding material cultures of geopolitics deserve greater attention. A deeper analysis would consider more the shape, form, and texture of objects and how these material qualities are pivotal to geopolitics and geopolitical relations. Populist leaders are often eager for fellow citizens to buy domestic products and ignore imported goods. Buying British or American or French products such as cars and food can become significant at moments of geopolitical and geo-economic stress. Purchasing becomes an expression of patriotism. Economic nationalisms are premised on certain geographical understandings of the world; domestic jobs need protecting from foreign labour and international investment and citizens need to favour locally produced products in order to support 'the people'. 'Foreign objects' might, as a consequence, attract expressions of anger and even destructive rage.

You never know, in other words, when geopolitics might sneak into our lives.

Postscript

Geopolitics in the 21st century is likely to be shaped by a series of pressures affecting all states and communities including: population growth (at least ten billion by 2100), resource consumption, climate change, and inequality. Beyond these mega-trends, some of the central tenets of the international system are being 'hollowed out'. Nation states struggle to exercise sovereignty over their national territories, as the distinction between inside and outside is hard to maintain let alone identify. The globalized patterns of politics, labour, culture, economy, and information make it very difficult to align with the protection and preservation of national cultures and clear-cut territorial borders. Populist forms of geopolitics are unquestionably a response to these geographical challenges, but there are others such as resisting demands for more collective action in the face of climate change.

President Trump's decision to withdraw from the 2015 Paris Agreement was premised on the assumption that this agreement might be economically disadvantageous to the United States. For critics, however, any commitment to a more progressive form of environmental geopolitics means acknowledging that humans have for too long treated nature as a series of cheap resources, which has enabled tremendous social-economic change in a largely unsustainable and destructive manner. The ecological services of the earth have enabled multiple expressions of geopolitical power—from energy extraction to food production and industrialization.

So, making sense of this shifting sense of geopolitics is going to require understanding how formal, practical, and popular expressions of geopolitics operate at multiple scales, address a huge array of issues, find expression on a diverse range of sites, shift over time, and feature in everyday life as well as the formal corridors of power. How we analyse and make sense of geopolitics reveals a great deal about how we feel, experience, and listen to the world around us.

Whether we like it or not, all of us are producers, dealers, and receivers of geopolitics.

References

Chapter 1: What is geopolitics?

T. Marshall, *Prisoners of Geography* (Penguin, 2015).

D. Massey, *For Space* (Sage, 2005).

W. R. Mead, 'The Return of Geopolitics', *Foreign Affairs* (May/June 2014) https://www.foreignaffairs.com/articles/china/2014-04-17/return-geopolitics (accessed 17 April 2019).

J. Seahill, *Dirty Wars: The World is a Battlefield* (Nation Books, 2013).

E. Said, *Orientalism* (Penguin, 1978).

Chapter 2: Intellectual poison?

I. Bowman, 'Geography v. Geopolitics', *Geographical Review*, 32 (1942), 646–58.

R. O'Brien, *End of Geography* (Routledge, 1992).

G. Ó Tuathail, *The Geopolitics Reader* (Routledge, 2006), 1.

F. Sondern, 'The Thousand Scientists behind Hitler', *Readers Digest*, 6 (1941), 23–7.

E. Walsh, *Total Power* (Doubleday, 1948), 21.

H. Kissinger, *The White House Years* (Little, Brown, 1979), 598, and his comments about Chile are available at: http://en.wikipedia.org/wiki/Chilean_coup_of_1973 (accessed 17 April 2019).

G. Chesney, *The Battle of Dorking* (Lippincott, Grambo & Co., 1871).

E. Childers, *Riddle of the Sands* (Smith, Elders & Co., 1903).

T. Mahan, *The Influence of Sea Power upon History 1660–1783* (Little, Brown & Co., 1898).

F. Ratzel, *The Sea as a Source of the Greatness of a People* (R. Oldenbourg, 1901).

S. Cohen, *Geography and Politics in a Divided World* (Oxford University Press, 1963).

T. Snyder, *Blood Lands* (Vintage, 2011).

Chapter 3: Architectures

J. Agnew, *Globalization and Sovereignty* (Rowan and Littlefield, 2017).

W. Brown, *Walled States, Waning Sovereignty* (MIT Press, 2014).

J. Nye, 'The Decline of America's "Soft Power"', *Foreign Affairs*, 83 (2004), 20.

D. Runciman, *How Democracy Ends* (Profile Books, 2018).

Chapter 4: Popular geopolitics

J. Agnew, *Making Political Geography* (Arnold, 2002).

W. Connelly, *Identity/Difference* (University of Minnesota Press, 2002).

Chapter 5: Identities

M. Billig, *Banal Nationalism* (Sage, 1995).

C. Ng, *Everything I Never Told You* (Blackfriars, 2014).

T. Paglen, *An Atlas of Radical Cartography* (Journal of Aesthetics and Protest Press, 2007).

Chapter 6: Objects

F. Cantú, *The Line Becomes a River* (Bodley Head, 2017).

D. Miller, *Stuff* (Polity, 2009).

Further reading

Much of the information relating to geopolitical matters available on the web is subject to great change and variation in quality. There are clearly UK and US publications, both print and online, that address matters of geopolitical interest such as *The Economist*, *The Spectator*, *New Statesman*, *The National Interest*, *The Atlantic*, *Prospect*, *Dissent*, *Foreign Policy*, and so on. Many of these magazines also support active blogs, and there are other online sources such as *Vox*, *Huffington Post*, *Politico*, *The Diplomat*, *The Hill*, *Slate*, and *Daily Kos*. Academic journals such as *Geopolitics*, *Territory, Politics and Governance*, and *Political Geography* regularly publish geopolitical analyses. There are some excellent introductions to choose from, including C. Flint, *Introduction to Geopolitics* (Routledge, 2016) and for a more classical expression, J. Black, *Geopolitics and the Quest for Dominance* (Indiana University Press, 2015).

More generally, search engines such as Google provide ample opportunities to explore the term geopolitics further, mindful of the fact that there are rich engagements of geopolitics outside the Anglophone world.

Chapter 1: What is geopolitics?

J. Agnew, *Globalization and Sovereignty* (Rowman and Littlefield, 2017).

D. Armitage, *Foundations of Modern International Thought* (Cambridge University Press, 2013).

J. Black, *Geopolitics and the Quest for Dominance* (University of Indiana Press, 2015).

D. Dixon, *Feminist Geopolitics* (Routledge, 2016).

K. Dodds, M. Kuus, and J. Sharp (eds), *The Ashgate Research Companion to Critical Geopolitics* (Ashgate, 2013).

C. Enloe, *Bananas, Beaches and Bases: Making Feminist Sense of International Politics* (University of California Press, 2014).

C. Flint, *Introduction to Geopolitics* (Routledge, 2016).

G. Ó Tuathail, *Critical Geopolitics* (Routledge, 1996).

S. Smith and R. Pain (eds), *Fear: Critical Geopolitics and Everyday Life* (Routledge, 2016).

Chapter 2: Intellectual poison?

M. Bassin and G. Pozo (eds), *The Politics of Eurasianism: Identity, Popular Culture and Russia's Foreign Policy* (Rowman and Littlefield 2017).

B. Blouet, *Halford Mackinder* (University of Texas Press, 1987).

I. Bowman, *The New World* (World Company, 1921).

S. Cohen, *Geopolitics: The Geography of International Relations* (Rowman and Littlefield 2014).

K. Dodds and D. Atkinson (eds), *Geopolitical Traditions* (Routledge, 2000).

T. Garton Ash, *Free World* (Random House, 2004).

P. Giaccaria and C. Minca (eds) *Hitler's Geographies* (University of Chicago Press 2016).

D. Haraway, *Primate Visions* (Routledge, 1989).

G. Kearns, *Geopolitics and Empire: The Legacy of Halford Mackinder* (Oxford University Press, 1998).

S. L. O'Hara and M. Heffernan, 'From Geo-strategy to Geo-economics: The "Heartland" and British Imperialism before and after Mackinder', *Geopolitics*, 11/1 (2006), 54–73.

G. Parker, *Geopolitics: Past, Present and Future* (Pinter, 1998).

W. Parker, *Mackinder: Geography as an Aid to Statecraft* (Oxford University Press, 1982).

J. Sharp 'A Subaltern Critical Geopolitics of the War on Terror: Postcolonial Security in Tanzania', *Geoforum*, 42 (2011): 297–305.

Chapter 3: Architectures

J. Agnew, *Hegemony: The New Shape of Global Power* (Temple University Press, 2005).

J. Agnew and S. Corbridge, *Mastering Space* (Routledge, 1995).

O. Bullough, *Moneyland* (Profile Books, 2018).

P. Dicken, *Global Shift* (Sage, 2014).

T. Friedman, *The World is Flat* (Farrar, Straus and Giroux, 2005).

G. Gong, *The 'Standard of Civilization' in International Society* (Oxford University Press, 1984).

D. Harvey, *A Brief History of Neoliberalism* (Oxford University Press, 2007).

S. Krasner, *Sovereignty: Organised Hypocrisy* (Princeton University Press, 1999).

P. Mirowski, *Never Let a Serious Crisis Go to Waste: How Neo-Liberalism Survived the Financial Meltdown* (Verso, 2013).

S. Nye, *Soft Power* (Public Affairs, 2004).

N. Smith, *American Empire* (University of California Press, 2003).

M. Steger, *Globalization: A Very Short Introduction* (Oxford University Press, 2017).

J. Stiglitz, *Globalization and its Discontents* (Penguin, 2017).

R. Wilkinson and K. Pickett, *The Spirit Level: Why Equality is Better for Everyone* (Penguin, 2010).

Chapter 4: Popular geopolitics

G. Agamben, *State of Exception* (Chicago University Press, 2005).

R. Bleiker (ed.), *Global Visual Politics* (Routledge, 2018).

S. Carter and K. Dodds, *International Politics and Film* (Columbia University Press, 2014).

F. Debrix, *Tabloid Terror: War, Culture and Geopolitics* (Routledge, 2007).

D. Holloway, *9/11 and the War on Terror* (Edinburgh University Press, 2008).

M. Power and A. Crampton (eds), *Cinema and Popular Geopolitics* (Routledge, 2006).

R Saunders and V. Strukov (eds) *Popular Geopolitics* (Routledge, 2018).

J. Sharp, *Condensing the Cold War* (University of Minnesota Press, 2000).

T. Snyder, *The Road to Unfreedom* (Bodley Head, 2018).

C. Weber, *I am an American: Filming the Fear of Difference* (Intellect, 2012).

Chapter 5: Identities

M. Billig, *Banal Nationalism* (Sage, 1995).

G. Dijkink, *National Identity and Geopolitical Visions* (Routledge, 1996).

M. Doel, *Geographies of Violence* (Sage, 2017).

D. Gregory, *The Colonial Present* (Blackwell, 2004).

S. Huntington, 'The Clash of Civilisations', *Foreign Affairs*, 72 (1993), 22–49.

G. Matthews and S. Goodman (eds), *Violence and the Limits of Representation* (Palgrave Macmillan, 2013).

D. Moisi, *The Geopolitics of Emotion* (Bodley Head, 2009).

E. Said, 'The Clash of Ignorance', *The Nation* (22 October 2001).

A. Smith, *Chosen Peoples* (Oxford University Press, 2003).

Chapter 6: Objects

A. Barry, *Material Politics: Disputes along the Pipeline* (Wiley-Blackwell, 2013).

J. Bennett, *Vibrant Matter: A Political Ecology of Things* (Duke University Press, 2010).

J. Dittmer *Diplomatic Material* (Duke University Press, 2017).

D. Gregory and A. Pred (eds), *Violent Geographies* (Routledge, 2006).

D. Miller, *Stuff* (Polity, 2009).

M. Monmonier, *How to Lie with Maps* (University of Chicago Press, 1996).

S. Turkle (ed.), *Evocative Objects: Things We Think With* (MIT Press, 2011).

Index

N

national identity 98–105, 110–16
National Security Agency
    (NSA) 11–12
    PRISM 11–12
national security cinema 79–84
NATO 23, 32–3, 60–1
Nazi Germany 16–30, 41–3
neo-conservatives 32
neo-liberalism 63–4
North Korea 3, 8–9, 75
Novichok 1

O

Occupy Movement 56–7, 64–5
origins of geopolitics 17–23

P

Pakistan 32, 35, 49–50, 103–4, 134
Palestine 105, 109–10
pan-regional identity 19–20, 99,
    106–12
Philippines 73
pipelines 127–30
Poland 24, 49, 108–9
popular culture 11–14, 37–8,
    72–3
    see also media
popular geopolitics 74–9, 91–7
    see also media
populism 63–4, 70
Portugal 22, 117
post-Columbian era 18–19, 53–4
practical geopolitics 71, 146
PRISM see under National
    Security Agency
Putin, Vladimir 3–4, 39, 47

Q

Qutb, Sayyid 118–19

R

race 31, 36–7, 99, 104–5
Reader's Digest 15–16
Reagan, Ronald 139–40
resources 3–4, 9, 17, 28, 61–2, 69,
    125–6, 145–6
Roosevelt, FD 16–17, 19–20, 60
Russia 1–3, 18–19, 35, 39, 42, 60–1,
    73, 75, 96, 128–9, 137
    see also Soviet Union

S

Said, Edward 116–17
SAP 61–2
September 11, 2001 terrorist
    attacks on United States
    (9/11) 119–20
    see also War on Terror
    civilizations 109–10, 117–18
    identity 98, 105
    internet 88–91, 93–5
    media 85
    State of the Union address
    2002 35
Serbia 106, 110–11
Snowden, Edward 11–12, 95
South America 24–5, 41–3, 102
South China Sea 7, 133
sovereignty 1–2, 14, 46, 49–58,
    102, 123–5, 133, 145
Soviet Union 2–3, 15, 23, 25–7,
    29–30, 32, 52–3, 80–2,
    126, 128
    see also cold war; Russia
    collapse of 62, 111–12, 117
    Third World 5, 29–30,
    32–3, 52–3
    United States 15, 29, 60, 62, 80
Spain 112–16
Sri Lanka 98, 115–16
Strausz-Hupe, Robert 27
subnational identity 99, 112–16

ONLINE CATALOGUE
A Very Short Introduction

Our online catalogue is designed to make it easy to find your ideal Very Short Introduction. View the entire collection by subject area, watch author videos, read sample chapters, and download reading guides.

http://fds.oup.com/www.oup.co.uk/general/vsi/index.html

SOCIAL MEDIA
Very Short Introduction

Join our community
www.oup.com/vsi

- Join us online at the official Very Short Introductions
  Facebook page.
- Access the thoughts and musings of our authors with our
  online **blog**.
- Sign up for our monthly **e-newsletter** to receive information
  on all new titles publishing that month.
- Browse the full range of Very Short Introductions online.
- Read **extracts** from the Introductions for free.
- Visit our library of **Reading Guides**. These guides, written by our
  expert authors will help you to question again, why you think
  what you think.
- If you are a teacher or lecturer you can order inspection
  copies quickly and simply via our website.